PRAISE FOR *A LIFE LIKE ANYBODY ELSE*

"Michael Long has been a visionary pioneer forging dreams of a future where people with disabilities are living, working, learning, and playing in communities that recognize the value of all people. He is an outspoken, courageous leader and 'hero' in the self-advocacy movement ... Michael's greatest gift is his simple humanity and honesty."
— Laura L. Larson, *Executive Director, State Council of California Developmental Disabilities Board*

"Wonderful ... informative and inspirational ... It really gives (readers) a different perspective."
— Barbara E. Bromley, Ph.D., *California State Polytechnic University, Pomona*

"Michael has made presentations in my Mainstreaming and Special Education classes for a number of years. I cannot praise Michael's contributions enough ... He is an example of the results for which we all strive."
— Patricia M. Phipps, Ph.D., *California State University, Chico*

"Michael Long tells the truth in this book. And truth about what it means to be a human being is hard to come by."
— Nancy R. Thaler, *Deputy Secretary for the Office of Developmental Programs, Commonwealth of Pennsylvania*

A Life Like Anybody Else

How a Man with an Intellectual Disability
Fulfilled His American Dream

THE MICHAEL S. LONG STORY

By Michael S. Long
as told to Karl Williams

Copyright © 2020 Michael S. Long and Karl Williams

Published by Michael S. Long

All rights reserved. No part of this publication may be reproduced, stored in a retrieval system, or transmitted, in any form or by any means, electronic, mechanical, photocopying, recording, or otherwise, without the prior written permission of the publisher.

Cover and book design by Mark Sullivan

Paperback: 978-0-9997422-9-7
E-book: 978-1-7335462-8-7

Printed in the United States of America

DEDICATION

I would like to be able to dedicate this book to my father,
Dudley Maxfield Long
(12/11/34 — 8/15/91)

I think it's really important to dedicate this book to him, to be able to have people read about what his son has accomplished, because he'd be out bragging it. That's one of the things he did great about us kids: He bragged about us so much. I think a lot of people who liked him — who knew him — will like this book.

Michael S. Long

CONTENTS

PREFACE
ix

EDUCATOR COMMENT
xiii

INTRODUCTION
xv

CHAPTER ONE | Farm and Family
1

CHAPTER TWO | Kindergarten, Grade School and Junior High
11

CHAPTER THREE | Freshman and Sophomore Years
32

CHAPTER FOUR | Junior and Senior Years
42

CHAPTER FIVE | Working on the Farm
58

CHAPTER SIX | The Bay Area
66

CHAPTER SEVEN | Chico
78

CHAPTER EIGHT | People First
98

CHAPTER NINE | Forging the Dream
106

Chapter Ten | The American Dream Launched
130

PREFACE

I met Michael Long in Toronto at the Third International People First[1] Conference. He gave a speech in which he portrayed his idea of himself, in relation to the "normal" world and then to the world of disabilities, by means of several diagrams with interlocking circles. What struck me most about the speech was how it quite naturally applied to everyone in the audience alike, myself and people with disabilities and advisors to the various self-advocacy groups represented. He spoke about self-worth and how important that is in everyone's life. The world of disabilities he'd found himself in was just his particular obstacle. What he said about the need for establishing one's self-esteem applied clearly to everyone regardless of his or her situation in life.

Soon after that, when Michael was invited to Pennsylvania's statewide conference, I made it a point to be there — I wanted to hear him speak, again. Afterward I went up to shake his hand. I said I was very glad to have heard him speak once more. I told him how very good I thought he was at what he did and that I was very happy to know him as a fellow human being.

Several weeks later, out of the blue as it seemed to me, I got a call from him. He wanted to write a book and he wanted me to help him do it. I say "out of the blue" because, if Michael

---

1. People First is the name used by many self-advocacy groups in the US and Canada — self-advocacy being the work of people with intellectual disabilities for their civil rights.

knew my work at all, he knew several songs I had written for the self-advocacy movement (the songs that had gotten me invited to Toronto). I was just finishing work on a book with Roland Johnson, another leader in the movement, but how could he have known about that?

Well, he'd been invited to return to Pennsylvania to speak again and he would arrange to stay a few extra days, during which time we would begin recording the conversations that would become the rough material for this book. He had it all figured out: He would pay for the costs of transcribing the material, for the occasional phone call that would be necessary, and for postage.

Several months later, I was astounded to see he'd been planning this book in his mind for years. I turned on the tape recorder, and he launched into his life: This is what had happened in first grade, in second grade, in third, and fourth; fifth and sixth grades were a bit muddled, because the classes had been combined that year ... and so on.

Michael Long is an amazing man. I believe he is a picture of what the future could be for people with this disability. His parents were strong, determined people, and they passed these traits on to Michael. They refused to be trapped into educational and social service systems that would have condemned Michael to a life that would have given him little chance of becoming who he really is. Instead, they insisted that Michael would be treated no differently from their other children. Michael's life was difficult because of that decision, but it was the kind of difficulty that made him strong and from which he eventually reaped many benefits.

The way I explain things to myself is that this society — and for all practical purposes, these days, we might just as well say, the world — values four things: intellect, power, money, and physical beauty. You'll do well if you have at least one of those assets in abundance; you'll get by if you have a smattering of two or three of them. But people with developmental disabilities very often have none of these assets, and the world sees no value in anything else. Michael Long had first to convince himself that the world was wrong — that there were other things of value. This took him a long time. We live both in the world and in our own heads, and if the world tells us we are worthless, there is little comfort left to be had in our inner lives.

As I said, these four things are what the world values, but there's a whole universe outside this one we've constructed for ourselves. And Michael's story is about how he found his way out of the world's negativity about him and into a new way of being.

At the same time Michael Long gives us a very concrete idea of how people with this disability can fit into society right now. I've said this many times to Michael and it continues to be true for me: I'm glad I got hooked up with him. I'm glad because this book we worked on together is something I'm proud to have my name on. I'm glad because he can do things I am not capable of. I'm glad because I would not want to have gone through this life without knowing Michael Long.

My contribution to this book was to ask the questions I thought necessary to help Michael tell the story he had to tell, and then to arrange the material in the best way possible. I took great care to use only Michael's words. If you know Michael, you'll hear him speaking when you read this book.

Michael won't mind my telling you that he cried more than once during our taping. He's gotten very clear about who he is, and he's very comfortable — happy would be a better word — to be who he is. I wouldn't be at all surprised if his story brings a tear or two to your eyes, too. I won't be giving a whole lot away if I tell you, now, that everything turns out just fine in the end.

In fact, that's just Michael's point: No matter what your situation is, don't let anything stop you from finding out who you are and becoming that person as best you can, and your life will turn out just fine, too. If you are a person who doesn't happen to have developmental disabilities, well, that's okay too. Just be careful not to rub that twist of fate into anyone else's face.

You're going to like this book; you won't be able to help it. Just as you won't be able to help liking Michael Long if you meet him or get to hear him speak.

Karl Williams

EDUCATOR COMMENT

Michael shared his life story with all of its tenderness, honesty, humor, and insight. His words are tangible evidence of what it means to push painfully through barriers of resistance with commitment, resilience, and a vision of wanting more out of life than the world was ready to give. Michael survived an educational system not always capable of embracing students with learning challenges. His story is a pleasure to read; the reader moves between smiles, laughter, and tears with every page and ends up contemplating about how, for most of us, our complaints are really quite petty and inconsequential.

Teresa Davis, Ph.D.
Professor Emerita
Special Education Programs
California State University, Chico

INTRODUCTION

We are not retards. We are people just like you.
 It was May 16, 1962, when I was born, right after midnight. Many dreams were shattered in the situation where my mom and dad were having a different son. He was not going to be capable of doing things. I was a big, breach baby, and I had the umbilical cord wrapped around my throat. I lost a lot of oxygen when I was born, and that formed a mild case of cerebral palsy and mental retardation — brain damage — from the lack of oxygen. I was put right in the incubator when I was born.

The doctor said, "You're going to have a child that's going to have a difficult time. He'll probably be nonverbal, not able to communicate."

But my mom and dad wanted to be able to keep me at home and be able to raise me at home. So my parents decided to bring me home and raise me like anybody else.

CHAPTER ONE

FARM AND FAMILY

I remember us kids laying down in the shed, going to sleep on top of the walnuts in the bins with the dryer blowing hot air through the walnuts. Mom and Dad worked around the clock, twenty-four hours. This was during the walnut harvest, October through November 1. The walnuts were our main crop; so that's the reason why we ran around the clock like that. Mom would bring us outside with her to keep an eye on us while she was working. My mother took care of the walnut dehydrator.

We always had a lot of fun lying down on top of the walnuts. The heat would rise up there, so it was always nice and warm. It's in a great big shed — it holds up to about fifty bins — and we have this great big blower that blows air underneath the bins. Here's how the walnuts are dried: The bins have metal on the bottom, and they have holes in that metal; so the dry air goes up through the walnuts, and that dries the walnuts. The blower is heated with propane gas to be able to blow the hot air underneath the tunnel where all the air goes up to heat the walnuts — to dry them off.

We were laying on top of the walnuts inside the bins where the hot air came up. The bin doesn't have nothing on top. We were laying on the walnuts — on top of themselves, and we kept warm by the warm air coming up underneath the tunnel. The blower dries about sixteen bins at a time, because there's three different sections, and each section has sixteen bins. It usually takes one to two days to dry the walnuts. After the walnuts are dried, then we have these big semi-trucks and we have a conveyor belt that runs in between.

You have your walls to protect the bin area and a walkway in between the bins. Underneath that walkway is a conveyor belt. When they're dry, we lift up this handle, and that opens up the bin, and all the walnuts come out. Then, they go up the conveyor belt into the semi-truck, and the semi-truck goes down to San Jose, California, and they're processed there.

We were in different bins. There was room for two people in the bins, but most of the time we wanted our own bin. The feeling — to describe it — it just felt so incredible, because you're all stretched out with all of these walnuts, and that hot air coming up to be able to keep you warm. Mom was always around those bins so she could keep working. Then, she would take us into the house.

What happens is that during December through, I would say, probably March, the trees are dormant, so there's no leaves or anything. The walnuts start as flowers and what we call a catkin. And a catkin is like a caterpillar ... it's hard to describe. Then, the catkin drops off and pollinates the flower, and then it forms a green husk. The green husk breaks apart, I would say, in the month of October or so. When they start doing that, it's time to start the walnut harvest. The walnut is taken off the tree by shaking the tree; then the walnuts fall down to the ground. What's left of the walnuts is just the walnut shell — like everyone knows about. If that green husk doesn't come off, that means the walnut is still too green.

I grew up on a farm of walnuts, and almonds, and prunes — about 400 acres of land. My dad and mom did a lot of commercial work — that's where a lot of the other people who owned orchards, we did their orchards for them. My father built the business up from a small twenty acres that he and his father bought, up all the way to 800 acres. We harvest over a thousand acres each year, including the commercial work. That took them about twenty years to be able to do that. That's where he really built his reputation up.

My brother Greg was the main one who always loved the farm; he really participated in every way he could — in everything — as he was growing up. He was the more active one of the family with the farm. I always hated the farm because I had to get up early in the morning. Us kids were always out there at 6 a.m. picking the prunes.

I remember my mom almost had a heart attack because she saw Greg when he was about ... I think it was about four years old ... driving the forklift out on the farm. He always had to be out there with Dad, moving the equipment, being a part of the action. Dad let him take the risk of driving the tractor around the yard — that was okay with my father. And it was okay for my mom too, but Mom was a little more scared of the situation than my father was.

Greg was the third one out of all of us. When Greg was born, I wanted him to be a horse; that did not work out. I wanted a horse so bad that my mom and dad got me this play horse — a wooden horse. That's where I rock back and forth. But I wanted a real horse.

I had a sister that was born in front of me, Nancy. She was one year older than I was — a year and two months. Then came me, and then came my brother, Greg, and then came my sister Kathy.

My older sister, Nancy, was always the one who protected me — always the one to make sure I was okay. I remember that somehow I got mad at her for something. I ended up scratching her face, and she has this tiny scar right down the middle. I got grounded for that, but Nancy always forgave me. She was the type of person who really stood up for everybody and really had a lot of fun doing it, too, I think. She also really loved to sing.

My younger sister, Kathy, was born on the day of the Red Bluff Rodeo Roundup. We were staying over at some friends' house, and Dad said, "You got a baby sister."

And I said, "I don't want a baby sister!"

I wanted a brother to be able to play baseball and basketball with. 'Cause Greg was so wrapped up in the farming, I didn't have anyone to really play with. It took a couple of years to get over it. Then I said, "Hey, I can do the things I wanted to do with my brother with her."

When she was about four years old, Kathy and I always went out and played basketball together — the hoops. We played one-on-one, Horse, Ring-Round-The-World. During the springtime we always got our bats and balls, and I went out and pitched softball to her. Kathy just really developed: volleyball, basketball, and track and field were her things. In high school, she won a bunch of awards for her athletic ability. In fact, her whole room at my parents' house is just full of trophies and little plaques and the little medals she won — and it just was by being committed to her sports.

One of the things I really admire about all of my siblings is that they didn't get an ego — that pridefulness stayed out of it. Kathy is one of the most down-to-earth people; Nancy, with her singing, is one of the most down-to-earth people, too, that anyone could be able to meet. You do not see this pridefulness. They have been able to keep that separate, and I think one of the reasons why they have been able to keep it separate is because of the parents we had. They taught us that you shouldn't get an ego. You should not get a prideful attitude about things, of your successes and everything. If you'd go the way that we went — with building our business on the basis of unpridefulness and honesty and being able to be trusted — you're gonna be able to make it in today's world situation. I think Mom and Dad laid the foundation for all of us kids; then we did the rest of the work.

We had a very small house to begin with. It was a living room with a porch, a small kitchen, a bathroom, and a small bedroom downstairs. It had an upstairs, and we had two bedrooms up there. One of the things that happened is, starting in I believe 1974, my mother and my father decided to add on and start making the house they wanted to have — as a family. So what happened is they knocked the porch out, and that became the living room — a great big living room type of situation, then the living room that was already there became the dining room. We had the kitchen still, and then we had the upstairs.

My grandfather was a carpenter and built houses. They used to live in a little town called Chico, which is thirty-five miles south of Red Bluff. When my father was in fifth grade, my grandfather decided to move up to the Red Bluff area. They moved into the house I grew up in — on twenty acres. From that twenty acres, my father decided to make a commitment that he was going to be a farmer the rest of his life; so he started borrowing money from the bank and buying different orchards. That's how he started out. He wanted to be able to build his business up. He was a master at being able to negotiate and how to be able to be fair on the bottom line. The most important thing about my father is that he did not want to cheat anybody out of anything. If he saw something that was cheating, he wouldn't do it. It was just really incredible in the way he mastered his own business situation.

My mother grew up in Chehalis, Washington, on a little farm. She always picked strawberries during the summer. That was her summer job, and she always saved money. She always worked on some kind of farm, but her goal in life was to be a teacher. She moved from Washington to California after graduation from college to be able to help her mother, because her mother was in California and was not doing well. And she settled in Red Bluff, and she met my father at a church function. It was love at first sight. Back in 1959 is when they got married. She was a teacher for three years at Red Bluff High School right before she got pregnant with me; then after I was born, she gave up teaching and just became a housewife. Then, after a housewife, she ran the farm with Dad. They were both Christians, so they were very committed in their relationship with God.

When I was a baby, I remember my father — in the sixties. Before they come up with what we called irrigation pipes and sprinklers, we used to flood irrigate. The whole orchard had to be disced up into a canal type of situation so water could reach certain areas throughout the whole orchard. It would probably be like half an acre at a time to be able to have water all over the ground. My father would lay down at night, because you would flood irrigate at like 2 a.m. in the morning, and he would lay down and he would sleep out in the field. What happened is he would lay down in the canal ditch, and then the water rose high enough and hit him in the face and that would tell him to get up and move on to the next section — to unshovel for the next little half an acre.

During part of the year we have what we call "frost protection" where the almonds are out in bloom. My father was a man who had to get up whenever the frost alarm went off. Usually they set it at thirty-five, and the freezing temperature is thirty-two. What we did ... he always woke people up — all the workers that worked for us — and we had to go out and light what we called "smudge pots." They were a round barrel type of thing full with diesel, and then you light it to be able to keep the tree warm — to protect the nuts and the blooms. We always went out and lighted those things by hand. Every minute counted, because it's getting cold. This is how we provide for our family.

Everyone loved my father because he really always gave. He gave his time to his kids, and he was a man that always was trusted by everybody because of the way he presented himself — the way he did business when he made contracts with other farmers. He was a guy who would always not look out for himself, who could settle for anything in negotiation. He always gave to people; he let people borrow a lot of equipment.

A couple of the places that my father and my mom bought over the years had houses on the property; so they have always let some of the workers that were year-round to be able to stay there ... staying in the homes. That way they could be able to get ahead for themselves. They never charge 'em any rent, so it was part of the benefits situation — that if you stayed with us all year round, you got a house. During harvest, I would say, there was about thirty people all together that worked, but then we only kept about six people all year round.

We had a lot of great workers — a lot of great people. It was a really big thing for my father to administrate that and, on top of it, do everything else. He was a man who was very committed to work and very committed to his family — to his wife — making sure there was enough for everybody in the family. He went the extra mile to make sure things did not break down.

Oh, wow, was he emotional — very emotional man. Every Saturday he liked to come in and watch *Wide World of Sports*, and if anyone did something terrific, he'll always end up crying at the end. That's how emotional he was, and that's where I get my emotion. I take after my father one hundred percent. There's no doubt about it. And I look exactly like him, too — people always have said that.

He always was out working. He always hated to take vacation trips, because he always worried about how the farm was. My father was a volunteer fireman. Oh, I remember that stupid scanner went off every night — that stupid blasted thing. They had to test everybody's scanner to see if it worked. It goes, BEEEEEEEP, BOOOONK, BEEEEEP, BOOOOOONK, BEEEEEEEP, BOOOOOONK! They'd do that every freaking night at six o'clock — at dinner time. BEEEEEEP, BOOOOOONK, BEEEEEP, BOOOOOONK, BEEEEEEP. THIS IS A TEST, ENGINE NUMBER 707, DO YOU HEAR US? And then there was a button to be able to click ... every night at six o'clock.

Our engine was Number 707; it was just down the road from ... it would be like right across the street in the city block, but it was like a fourth a mile from our house.

And man, Dad, he was great. He loved this stuff. It scared the heck out of me. I remember I yelled at him. I said, "Dad! There's a thing on Such and Such Boulevard or Avenue."

He said, "Okay. Thanks, Mike!"

He'd just tear right out of there — ran. He had to jump into the truck. EEEEERRR. You heard that rubber burning all the way down to the fire station. That's why people liked him so much — because when there was ever a 'mergency situation, he was there. I mean, he was really there.

I remember I rode a couple of times, but ... liability issues and all of that kind of stuff. He gave me rides in the fire trucks when they had to refill them up with water after a fire. It was barns and houses and medical heart attacks and people having accidents ... Oh, my father saved many lives, many lives.

Mom ... she is a most incredible person that you could ever imagine. She's like my father ... just exactly like my father. She worked awful hard her whole life — the most giving person, the most giving.

Mom was always involved. That's the kind of couple they were, very committed to each other. They really let each other know what the other one was doing. That's what makes a marriage work — letting other people know what you're doing. At times, Dad had different opinions than Mom. Dad might have taken a risk here and there — of not getting approval with Mom — but later on they worked together to understand each other, why they did this or that. They always came up with a mutual agreement of not being mad at each other — at all. There's always the love and support. I never ever saw any time or any situation where my mother and father got into an argument in front of us kids; it was always private and reserved. That's the kind of environment that we grow up in. In today's society, you don't see that very often.

* * *

When I was born, the doctor also said, "He may not be able to walk in his life." So when I went home, the doctor was saying, "Notice when he starts crawling ... walking ... "

So my parents looked for those steps. When I was about two and a half, my parents started noticing that I was having a very difficult time with balance and learning how to walk. My mother and dad took me to Children's Hospital in Oakland, California. When we went in, we saw a bunch of specialists — pediatricians. From Red Bluff it was a three-and-a-half-, four-hour drive to Oakland.

I remember one of the times I was in my undershorts, and I didn't have any robe on. I had to go out in the hallway, and I had to do some certain things out in the hallway — I had to show the doctor how I could crawl and walk. There were people standing out in the hallway, and they were sitting in the hallway. I always fell down; I couldn't coordinate. And that always embarrassed me, not having a robe. After that, we were able to start receiving some therapy in Red Bluff ... working on my leg muscles.

I was having a hard time being able to pronounce my words. I wasn't saying the words that Mom and Dad loved to be able to hear; so my mother and my father started looking around for a speech therapist. It was in the sixties, when services were not very available. When I was three, my mother found a speech therapist in Chico — about a forty-five-minute ride. He tried to get me to say things like "banana," but I just wouldn't do it. My mom decided it was too long a drive, so we stopped.

We started to do therapy at home, and I started building up my leg muscles. When I was five years old, my parents had to be able to make a choice: Where should Michael go to school? Should Michael go to a school where all people with developmental disabilities go to, or should Michael go to a school where his brothers and sisters go? What happened is ... Michael's parents decided to try me out at the public-school system, instead of the segregated school system.

CHAPTER TWO

KINDERGARTEN, GRADE SCHOOL AND JUNIOR HIGH

I always remember one of the things I loved so much about kindergarten was there was milk and cookies. I always ended up taking my neighbor's cookies and drinking other people's milk. Also another thing ... we had this little sandbox that we played in. I ended up having a specific corner of the sandbox, and I didn't want no one to be able to get in that corner. I ended up always grabbing a handful of sand, and if anyone came around that territory, they'd get a handful of sand in their face. The reason why I flunked kindergarten, I thought, was because I was just a misbehaved child — because I threw sand at people's face, and I stole milk and cookies.

The principal suggested I go to a segregated school, but my kindergarten teacher was a really prime advocate. She told my parents, "Don't you even dare put him in a class like that. You're going to lose a son completely."

That helped them make the decision to protect my education. The school district didn't really like that.

* * *

One of the things the doctor recommended is when I go to school, they start taking me out of class to work on therapy and being

A LIFE LIKE ANYBODY ELSE

able to have me work on balance more. I went on to first grade and what happened is … they always took me out of the classroom. That created a bunch of walls in between me and my peers because they wanted to know why Michael always got to leave out of the class, and why they didn't get to leave, and what special treatment does Michael have over us. That created a lot of barriers.

The therapists were very hard to find — very difficult to find. In fact, the school district contracted out with the county school district to be able to get a speech therapist to come out there Monday, Wednesday, and Friday. They started noticing cognitively that I was having a hard time being able to remember things. I was about six years old at that time, and I was being pulled out of class.

The school psychologist always wanted to find out what was wrong with Michael, and why he was always behind with things. When the psychologist took me out, he wanted to give me the IQ tests. At that time, I didn't know what it was. I didn't even know what an IQ was. We played with these blocks — part of the testing was to be able to play with blocks and put them in order. I always hated playing with these blocks. Also, I noticed this little round clock, not a clock, this little round thing that had a button on top. What would happen is after I'd try to organize the blocks, I saw the psychologist click this button down. The button had a bunch of numbers on it — twelve buttons: one, two, three, four, five, six, seven, eight, nine, ten, eleven, and twelve. At the time, I didn't know it was a stopwatch to be able to time you on certain things. All I knew was it was a round thing with numbers and a button. It really irritated me that he had this little thing where this hand went around, and he clicked it all the time when I was trying to put the blocks together. I couldn't understand what he was doing.

What frustrated me more in the situation was ... he had this piece of paper, and he always would mark something down on that piece of paper. At that time, I didn't know what it was, but now I know that was the score of how I did on my IQ and, cognitively, what was wrong with me. That really kind of scared my dad — in a way.

What my father was scared of was the psychologist testing, of putting me in the segregated school, because the test score shows I don't belong at the general education school. So my father decided to run for the school board and be able to protect my education and work within the system. So he advocated from within.

One of the things my father did every morning ... his favorite restaurant was Denny's, and he always met the other farmers at Denny's for coffee in the morning. They always talked about the gossip in town and everything. So he always was talking to other farmers, and to other people, and to the community at large.

Dad and Mom always watched the news. In fact, Dad, when he came in for lunch, he always had the twelve o'clock news on. Always. We hated it as kids. Well, my father was a politician himself — being on the advisory board of FFA, and all of that kind of stuff. FFA — that's Future Farmers of America. It's like a 4H group at the high school level here in California, because this is one of the biggest agriculture areas. And also back in the Midwest they have a lot of them. What happens ... it's a course through the high schools. If you wanted to be a farmer and find out what it's like to be a farmer, you would take that course.

Yeah, he was into politics all the time. They always went out and voted. It was the thing to do — to go out and cast your ballot. That was really important to my family.

In California you have to have term limits if the population is over 100,000. In our area, we didn't have population that was over a hundred-thousand people; therefore we didn't have term limits on our school board. Dad got voted in all the time. He got voted in all the time, so he protected my education all the way through, through my elementary years and junior high years.

He was on the ballot every four years. When his term was up, he went out and he got elected again. He did his campaigning by farming. He'd go and help out other people ... talk to other people. People voted for him because he was so well-known.

He was very influencing on the situation. He had a really strong belief that his child should not be treated any different than anybody else, and he's going to grow up just like everybody else does. On the school board, he always made sure we always had the necessary things — like the therapy and the speech therapist and all of that to help me out, and other people to be helped out of what they needed.

He was really conservative, also. There had to be enough people for services to be able to spend the money type of situation. He also really made sure the school was running the right way — not running in the deficit — and maintaining the quality programs.

First grade at Lassen View, I made it through, but it was a struggle situation. I remember the first time I heard the word "mentally retarded" was in first grade. It wasn't from my parents; it was in first grade when everyone called me "retardo." I didn't know what it meant, but I didn't like the word. I hated the word "retarded." I didn't have no meaning of it at all — no comprehension of it. I don't think I really comprehended it 'til I was about in high school ... really understand what it was.

* * *

And second grade came along. This was so great. I was so excited one day. I decided to dress up in the suit I had, and I didn't want any of my family members to see me. We didn't live too far away from the school — it was down the street. I don't know how many miles, exactly. It was ... it was closer than into Red Bluff. We lived way out in the country about eight miles from Red Bluff.

I usually took the bus, but that day I felt like walking to school — taking the risk of walking — which was part of my therapy program. I decided to sneak out the back door, which used to be the old living room door and now was the dining room door. I snuck out the back door, and on the way I grabbed this toy ring that I had from out of a gumball machine. Then, I went ahead and picked some flowers in the back yard on the way to school. I had a crush on this girl. She was a second-grader like I was, and I was really excited about the situation that I was going to school in the suit, and I was bringing a ring, and I was bringing flowers. I was looking for her — her name was Jill.

I finally found her, and I said, "Jill! How are you?"

She said, "Fine. How are you doing?"

I said, "Jill, I'm doing great! I want to be able to ask you to marry me — today. Here's the flowers. Here's the ring. Let's go off and get married on the playground."

She was so shocked and smiley and didn't even say yes or no. When the bell rang, I went in and the teacher got involved after that. The teacher pulled me inside and said, "Michael, you got two minutes!"

What she was saying was, "You give me two minutes to be able to go get the principal to cover the class. You stay where you're at for two minutes while I go get the principal."

I said, "Yes."

She went ahead and did that, and she said, "You understand what marriage is about?"

Here I was like seven or eight years old, and I didn't know what marriage is about and things like that.

She said, "Well, Michael. It's about love and commitment and understanding. You gotta give and take in marriage. The most important thing that you gotta have is money for you can support yourself, and when you have a family, it's a big job."

I said, "Well, that is a big job."

I related how I comprehend that because of my parents being able to work all the time ... that's how I related the issue to that moment.

She said, "Michael, there's something else that I want to be able to tell you about."

I said, "What's that?"

She said, "Michael, your IQ is too low, and you're too mentally retarded. You'll never get married in your life."

That really set up a new belief system inside of me: that I couldn't associate with anybody who was different than me; where I thought everyone else in my classroom thought I was different — weird; that I couldn't handle anything, that everyone wanted me to be isolated — not be a part of the classroom. Not only that I had a belief system like that, but I had an image of myself that I was weird; I was different and I couldn't hang out with anybody else; that I was too mentally retarded to be able to have any friends to be able to associate with on the playground.

That idea controlled my life all the way through my elementary and junior high years. The belief system lasted up until I was about twenty-four years old. I did not tell a soul about the situation.

* * *

I went ahead past second grade, and third grade came on. I got homework, too. I had to do homework. My mom would work with me. I even went to summer school. We had a teacher who taught summer school for reading, so I always went to a reading class during summer. It was always two hours a day during the summer where I read to a teacher and always kept up on things for I won't fall farther behind.

I went on living my third-grade life. I was still being pulled out for speech therapy and for physical therapy, and everyone was wondering why I got to be able to leave. It created a great big barrier in between classmates and myself.

I always was called the teacher's pet — that was my nickname throughout the whole school. The reason why I had that nickname is because I had the special assignments to do and not the general assignments that other people had. I was doing the same kind of things as everybody else would do, but it would be more simplified — where my comprehension level was at and memory levels. I always worked on reading. Reading was one of the main subjects that they really focused on throughout my elementary years. It was really a challenge, because I was treated a little bit different than everybody else was.

Third grade I remember I had to dress up as a clown for a Halloween carnival at the school. After the carnival, I decided to take the costume to school. Everyone thought I was weird and different — and I wanted all of this attention. So how I got attention in third grade was one day I decided to wear the clown suit to school. During lunch and during some of the recesses, I always had this clown outfit on, and I waved to everybody. Everyone came and wanted to be around me, because I was a clown.

* * *

At the bus stop all the kids always picked on me. It was always difficult to be able to go to catch the bus because of the harassment I received. The bus driver, he was my best buddy. It was all older people — my parents' age, other farmers — that were my friends and my pals. I never really had friends my age. It was very painful to go and catch the bus. Nancy was at the school with me, and that's where Nancy protected me. She was a very concerned sister ... very protective sister at the bus stop and at school.

If she said, "Knock it off," they would knock it off, because they know what would happen if they didn't knock it off. What would happen is ... the bus driver would find out about the situation, or one of the teachers, or the principal, or Mom and Dad would find out at home what was going on. Nancy was the one who really told Mom and Dad a lot of the stuff what happened. My Dad talked to a few neighbors about what was happening, and then the kids were better.

Mom and Dad treated me a little differently from what the other kids were treated. What was big-time was Mom wouldn't let Dad touch me. Dad wanted to shipshape me up when I was a kid. What I mean by shipshape me up is to be able to train me to grow up — not getting away with things.

I always end up sleeping a lot when I was little. That's why Dad didn't think I would amount to very much — because I always slept. I would say I was a troublemaker. At home I got away with a lot of other things. That made my brothers and sisters mad, because they didn't get away with it — special privileges and all of that. I think that created a barrier between my father and I, because Mom always stuck up for me. My mother wouldn't let him chew me out, or wouldn't let him spank me, or do any of that kind of stuff.

And all the other kids — I mean, we were never abused or anything like that, but you know, when a kid misbehaves, you train 'em. The way that you train 'em ... you ground 'em or you spank 'em or whatever.

Mom always stuck up for me in the situation of chores. My chore was being able to bring in the wood. That's how our house was heated — by two fireplaces. Where we got the firewood is from almond trees — that is one of the best woods that you ever can get. It doesn't create a lot of ashes, and it burns for a long time. With a wood stove, we only burned a half cord a week. We took out some almond orchards and we plant 'em into walnut orchards. That's the reason why we did that — when Dad bought 'em, and Mom bought 'em. These orchards were sixty, seventy years old, and an almond tree usually lasts up until, I would say, about eighty years old. The really good years of productivity is from six years to about forty — where you get good crops if you don't have frosts that kills the crop, and you don't have hail that ruins the crop.

Especially during the winter, that was the biggest chore — to bring in the wood. I always hated that because of the coordination and the problem of not being able to lift heavy wood. So it took much more longer time for me to fill up the wood box than the average person would take. And I always hated it. It was a dirty chore, and I didn't like doing it.

Mom wouldn't let me go out and do things — experience things. She was more afraid of people taking advantage of me. I was easy to take advantage of, so it was overprotectingness. I remember one time I was grounded, and Mom took off on a trip. Dad forgot all about me being grounded, so we had some friends come down from Redding.

I said, "Dad, can I go up and spend three, four days up with the Druses? They want me to come up."

"Sure. Why not? No problem. Go ahead."

Mom hit the roof when she found out I was up in Redding, because she had to come all the way up to Redding to pick me up. Then did I ever got a lecture on the way home.

I really didn't have as good a relationship with my mother or my father as I would like, because all three of us never grew up. They were controlling; so there was always the conflict. So what happened ... I had an attitude that I knew best what was for me. I developed that when I was, probably, two years old. I knew best and get out of my way. They had the parent, general attitude: We been through this situation before, so we know best. So we were not quite as close through elementary and junior high.

The only really friction at home was my brother and sisters said I got "special treatment." My sister Kathy, she was the one that really played with me at home; but it was such an age gap between us — I was in high school when she started school. I was eight years older, so there was no comparison. That's why Kathy really played a lot with me — basketball and everything.

Nancy, she had friends over. Greg never really had much friends over; Greg always went over to their houses. Greg's friends didn't get used to me until they grew up a little bit — after they got out of high school. It was because of the coordination, then lack of skill, and the lack of being able to comprehend what people were doing and that they were playing around. I couldn't do it with Greg or anybody, because they were much farther along with their capabilities than I was. So I was always left out.

I always hated the farm, because I had to get up early in the morning and we were, us kids, were always out there at 6 a.m. to start working and picking the prunes. We have a machinery that came by to shake the tree. What it is, is a great big machinery that has great big long arms, and then at the end of those arms they have two great big cushion pads. And what happens is that you drive up to the tree, and you open the arms up, and then those paddings grip the trunk of the tree and just shakes the heck out of 'em. All the prunes or the almonds come down onto the ground. With the prunes you have this tarp that you pull out around the tree, and all the prunes fall down on the tarp. Then you have this button that you push that rolls the tarps up. People hold on to the tarps as it rolls up to the conveyor belt. When the conveyor belt gets at the end, all the prunes go up into that belt and into the box. Us kids, what our job was, any prunes that were left around the tree, we had to go around with the bucket and pick 'em all up. That was our main responsibility of prune harvesting.

Then the almond harvest ... it was the next harvest for us. We always raked the almonds that was left out by this machine into a windrow. It's called the sweeper — that makes the windrow. We went ahead and did a lot of raking ... making sure that all the almonds get into the windrow for the machine to come by and pick up. We also had to pick out sticks in the windrow, for the sticks won't mess up the machinery that came up and picked up the walnuts or almonds. That was part of our responsibilities, too.

I want to tell you ... during prune harvest we were in the bathroom twenty-four hours just about. They get old after a while; prunes get old. You get tired of eating them.

I had the biggest crush on this babysitter that we had. Why we would have babysitters is because of being able to have my parents out in the orchards and everything when we were little kids. On the weekend there was always a babysitter around to help out during harvest.

This babysitter was something else. Her name was Lee, and I believe she was in high school when she was babysitting us. She always helped us out during the weekends. She was always a person that took care of us ... and make sure everything was in order and straight. She was my favorite babysitter out of all the babysitters we had. Lee was my favorite one. I always couldn't wait to see Lee the next weekend.

* * *

So fourth grade I lived through. I remember a story about fourth grade where my teacher always kept an eye on the situation, saying, "Michael, quit being a CW."

I always wanted to know what a "CW" was. She was a person who never had handled anyone with any special needs or with any developmental disabilities, ever before. She was a person who always had someone to be able to pick on in all her classes that she taught. Over the years she always picked out one person, and she always picked on me.

She was saying, "Michael, what I mean is quit being a clock-watcher. You're going to get your recess when the bell rings."

My feelings of what she was doing here was ... she was picking on me because I always was anxious to get out on the playground, or I always was anxious to be able to get home. How she made me feel, also, was really defensive — that I'm different than anyone else. Someone's picking on me. Someone's harassing me. Therefore I had feelings that I did not belong in the classroom.

* * *

Fifth grade was a year where we had a combination class of fourth, fifth, and sixth. It wasn't a good year. I didn't like fifth

KINDERGARTEN, GRADE SCHOOL & JUNIOR HIGH

grade. Why? I don't know. I just can't remember what happened in fifth grade.

I was in the band in sixth grade, seventh grade, and eighth grade. I played the drums. That was no big thing, you know. I was in the choir — I sang, but I didn't make a career out of it.

But in sixth grade ... oh, I was a big man now, because I was on the junior varsity football team. I always stand on the sidelines, though, because I wasn't coordinated or quick enough to really participate in anything, but I was out there.

In sixth grade I was on the junior varsity of the basketball team, too. I remember that we always have basketball tournaments, and I was always sitting on the bench and didn't even got to play in sixth grade. There were tryouts, but one of the things I always believed in — why I always got picked on the third string — is because everyone knew my dad because of being on the school board. I think that had a lot to do with the situation of being able to make the team — of being able to be a third-string person or a second-string person. I was right on the borderline in between second and third string.

* * *

Seventh grade I remember we had this great big meeting of my father, and my mother, and my teacher, and the psychologist. I was tested psychology each year — about four times a year. They always kept a rope on me. The teachers, all through my eighth-grade years, had to get along with me. They weren't happy about the situation.

They went ahead and had this great big meeting because ... *Michael is not capable of being here at this public school. Socially skills ... he's not surviving. He's falling through the cracks. We need to be able to develop a better program. He's barely making it through the school system.*

My father felt that he didn't care what this IQ stuff says. He didn't care what anyone thinks. His son was going to stay here at this school until he graduates. He said, "Lookit. He made it this far, and he's going to continue and graduate at this public school system."

That ended the meeting, so I continued on in the situation. Social-wise, I didn't really have any friends, even though my mother always had big birthday parties for me, and a lot of kids came.

The beginning of the sixth grade, Karen was one of the leaders in the class. Karen was one of those type of girls that had everything from the family. She was the one of this group to really influence the group of hating me.

Then it really got worse in the seventh grade. My parents took in two foster girls when I was in seventh grade. How this came about is ... their father wanted to make sure that his kids were taken care of. He came down to visit my family after severe heart problems and said he wanted to make sure his kids were taken care of. My parents agreed to take the kids if anything happened. Then, he had a heart attack and died. That's how it happened, so they lived with us for half of their lives. They're still part of our family today — I mean they count us as real family.

We knew these two kids. We stayed in contact ... always played with each other and everything. At the time that their father was ill, they lived about forty-five minutes north of Red Bluff, in Redding. Becky is the oldest one, and Becky was really close to Nancy. Nancy was her best, best friend. My oldest sister was a freshman, and the adopted sister was a freshman also.

In 1976 we decided to add on a great big family room — add on to where the kitchen and the dining room was. We added on out to the west of the house. We went ahead and put in a great big playroom-family-room type of thing. My father decided to get a ping-pong table and an air hockey table. And so then after that we decided to add on what we called a utility room, which is north of the house. It was stretched out, and we had our closets and our washer and dryer and everything out there. When we put that utility room in, we decided to put in another bathroom and so we had another bathroom. In the family-room-playroom-type-thing, we decided to add a little bathroom in there.

In 1977, when the two girls came and lived with us, upstairs we decided to add on another room, because my two sisters lived in one room upstairs, and my brother and I lived in another room upstairs. We knocked out a whole portion of this closet and made it into a hallway type of thing, then a room would go over the family room upstairs. Everyone slept upstairs, 'cept for Mom and Dad — they slept downstairs. That was the only bedroom downstairs. So when the girls came to live with us, we went ahead and added one more room, and we added a bathroom — a half bathroom. My father ... amazing funny thing about my father ... he said he had to be able to add that bathroom in there, because none of the guys could go to the bathroom, because all the girls — all my sisters — had every bathroom filled up all the time.

The two girls had to change schools and come to the schools where we were going to as a family. Barbara was the one my age. It was hard for me to adjust having Barbara come — or Becky, either of them — and live with us. The second thing was Barbara being in the same grade. She had a lot of friends. I didn't have hardly any friends in seventh grade or eighth because they all harassed me.

Nancy had started high school at that time, so she wasn't around. My seventh- and eighth-grade years were really difficult because I did not have anybody around to stick up for me in the situation. There was a lot of pain for Barbara, too. Her father just died and everything, and then she had to come to our place. It was Becky that was really close to Nancy. Barbara and I were not really close.

I think seventh and eighth grade is the most difficult years for anybody. Even if you don't have a developmental disability, it's really difficult. It was this competition situation between brother and sister — of trying to gain control of friendships — that made me feel rotten.

I understand my mother and father's idea behind it. If something happened to them, they would want someone to be able to take care of us, instead of having a state agency coming in to take us away. So there was a lot of pain for Barbara. Her father just died and everything. She didn't like to come to our place. She wanted to go to her friends, because she was not close to anybody. It was Becky that was really close to Nancy. Barbara and I were not really close. We never did connect with each other when we saw them in Redding. We never did click. I think seventh and eighth grade is the most difficult years for anybody. Even if you don't have a developmental disability, it's really difficult.

When people picked on me, I always end up clamming up — closing up. I always went to the teacher … talk to the teacher about it, and they would get on the classes about it. Then came the teacher's pet thing. I was the "TP" of every teacher. He or she was my security.

One of the people who always picked on me ... his name was Allen. Allen was one of the group of cheerleaders in the real popular crowd of Lassen View Junior High that we went to. My mom ended up going over to Allen's house one day and having a talk with Melinda — that's Allen's mom. Mom went over to talk about the way that the cheerleaders were treating me.

In the middle of the process with the two mothers talking, Allen came out his bedroom and said, "Mrs. Long, this is why we do this: We don't like Mike because he always gets treated special. We don't like the way that he's getting away with all the things that we don't get away with. If we had homework to be turned in the next day, Michael doesn't have to turn it in until two days after or three days after when it was due. This is why we harass him. We don't like him. He's retarded."

* * *

One of the things I remember about eighth grade was a neighbor of mine — her name was Sabrina. She didn't like me very much, because I was different and I was weird. I was out playing football on lunch recess, and we divided up on teams. One of the things I always hated about dividing up in teams ... you always have to get in the group situation, and there's always got to be a last one to be picked. I knew I was always going to be the last one to get picked. I didn't want to be the last one picked; I wanted to be at the top or at the middle. But I was always the last one picked in these type of situations.

What happened at this lunch recess is I went out for a pass. And I dropped it. Sabrina came up to me and she said, "You're retarded. You can't even catch a football. You don't belong here.

Why don't you go to the school with all the other retarded people? Why are you here with us? You don't belong here. Your parents are trying to stop you from going there, and I think you'd be better off going there."

I remember the next thing I decided to do is walk off, and the bell rang for fifth period. As I was walking off, next thing ... I was tackled, and I hit the ground. Then, a quick left came around and bust me in the nose. Blood was just coming out — pouring out of the mouth and nose and everything.

The next thing I remember is my hair was grabbed by this person, and she started banging my head up against the ground. She said, "You never walk away from me when I'm trying to talk to you."

It took five guys to get her off me. One guy tried to pull her off. I couldn't get away. And she was right back on top of me. Then, another guy pulled her off, then another guy pulled her off, and another. Finally, the teacher who was on yard duty showed up, and all this blood was just pouring all over the place.

It was one of the most embarrassing moments of my life, because a man got beat up by a woman out in the playground. It was really a difficult situation to handle, not only because a man got beat up by a woman, but it was difficult because of realizing that no one really wanted me to be at this school all these years.

It was difficult to go through the pain and the sorrow and the frustration of the name calling, and the harassment, and the barriers that the school's psychologist put on me by pulling me out of the classrooms, and the teachers giving me special assignments instead of other assignments. What always made me feel really bad is when report cards came out during my elementary years. I always never got a A, B, C, D, or an F. I always got an S+ or an S-.

That was really frustrating to me when I saw everyone else got A's and B's and C's, and I only got an S. What did "S" mean? What did "S+" mean? I'm different. Why am I different? All of these emotions through elementary school years really played on me.

Ted, he was another guy that always harassed me — always picked on me. He especially picked on me on the bus. I remember one day when the bus driver said to Ted to knock it off.

He said, "Hey, give that guy a opportunity, and he will show you what he can do. It might not be in a fist fight, it might not be able to be in sports, but you wait and see. Just give him a chance, and he will surprise you."

What Ted did was sat back and kind of watched for a couple of years. By the time eighth grade was over, Ted became my friend.

* * *

Mom and Dad was very conservative about sex; they never did any talking. It was hard. It was more hard for me because I had a developmental disability. That had a lot of things to do with anger and a lot of frustration. I didn't know what in the heck was going on. Why I was expressing all of this — trying to figure out why I had all these hormones and feelings and all of that kind of stuff. I just withdraw from it. Kept quiet about it.

* * *

I graduated in eighth grade, and I remember graduation was quite an experience for me. Here I was in the public-school system with everybody else. I was so excited that I get to walk down this long hallway, then out on a slab were chairs for the class. Off of the slab there was a great big open yard where the audience got to sit.

I remember that graduation was the time of being able to celebrate the pain and agony that I face as an individual. It meant that I'd gone through the first hurdle of my life. That was really important to my parents and to myself. When they called my name up to be able to get my diploma, I didn't understand what was going on. I got it. I received it. After I received my diploma, I went and sat down.

I remember we had a classmate read off some of the things that the classmates were going to be doing in the future, and how they were going to run into each other in the near future. I remember that my name wasn't on there — that I wouldn't be remembered. My name wasn't on the speech — part of what would happen ten, fifteen years after graduation — where we would run into each other, and they would own the businesses. It was imagination type of situation ... where the class will be ... where everyone would be in about ten to fifteen years after graduation. I remember I was not included.

Then, we had a eighth-grade dance. I remember at the dance that we sat around and cried — all of us. We didn't want to leave the place. Everyone was upset. Everyone was scared.

Everyone was amazed that they reached this far.

I remember that the principal of the school and eighth-grade teachers who were chaperoning the dance said, if we don't get with dancing, and if we don't quit crying, they were gonna call the dance off. I made sure I went out and danced. I ended up dancing, usually, by myself.

* * *

One of the things I believe in is that we should mainstream and integrate people with developmental disabilities. They need to be able to experience those type of experiences, because later on in life, those experiences are going to help them out. Yes, it was difficult to go through all those experiences, but every day is a difficult time for each and every one of us who lives in today's society.

CHAPTER THREE

FRESHMAN AND SOPHOMORE YEARS

Our junior high was with the elementary school — kindergarten all the way through eighth. I was fourteen years old, and I remember the counselor said, "Where do you want to go to school? Do you want to go to Red Bluff High, or do you want to go to a continuation school where other people with disabilities go?"

At that time, 1977, special education was formed in California. In 1977 the law was passed. I don't know the grassroots of how it got organized, or what was the purpose here in California. I don't know if there was a big push for it through parents. But I know in Red Bluff, in 1977, the high school started implementing it right away. We had a principal and a superintendent that really believed that it needed to be able to get off the ground right there and right now, and not have the feds come in or have the states come in and do investigations and put penalties on.

I thought I was gonna be able to get into mainstream through special education. I told the counselor, "I would like to go to Red Bluff High, because my sister's there."

And I said, "Really, the real reason why I want to go there is because I've always got picked on in my elementary years. I got so used to being picked on, that I think I should be picked on more."

She said, "Why do you think you should be picked on?"

I said, "Well, because that's my life — I get picked on!"

So they developed where I was taking four or five periods of special education, and the sixth period I was mainstreamed into PE. They thought I only could handle PE.

My father wanted to make sure I would not get taken advantage of in high school. He wasn't on the high school board. If I wanted to go to Red Bluff High, I gotta be in the special education department. He knows that kids take advantage of the situation if I was mainstreamed in a lot of classes, or if I just took general education courses. He thought I would have a much more difficult time of passing the courses; therefore, it was best to put me in special education — to make me succeed and get a diploma.

On high school campuses in California, we usually have a building separated from the campus that is the special education department — separated from the main campus. Why I have a hard time with that is because it becomes the "retarded section" when it's separate, and a we-don't-dare-cross-that-borderline situation.

Our special education department was right in the center of the campus. Woodshop was the building that was separated from the rest of the campus. I was fortunate enough not to experience that humiliarity — the agony of that situation — because we were in the center of the campus. I really think that if we want a true society of mainstreaming and integration, we need to be able to educate people with developmental disabilities in high schools, and junior highs, and elementary schools, and knock down the barriers.

I always remember being able to hear, "Don't walk down that hallway, because that's where the retards hang out!" And we always was treated differently than everyone else on the campus.

I was really grateful that Nancy was older than me. She was in high school two years before I was. She set the tone and the stage for me when I got up to the high school area — even though I was in special education. She talked about her brother being disabled and being different. She said, "When he come up here, we want to make sure he's included with everything."

She also talked to teachers, and she talked to the principal about me. She laid the path exactly the right way to be able to have it worked out for the first two years. Nancy was the type of a person that really stood up for everybody and really had a lot of fun doing it, too.

She was a person who really loved to sing. In fact she had a chance to go professionally, but she decided to have a family instead. That was really important. She had a very clear, crisp voice. I have not seen anyone who could make you so emotional when she's singing; she has that talent. She could grab people's hearts and just sock them down.

When she was in junior high, she played the saxophone — that was her thing. She had a lot of fun with playing the saxophone, but mainly it was singing that she really did. She was in a lot of choirs: school choir, the church choir, the choir at the high school when she was in high school. The Red Bluff choir got asked to go to a competition in Reno, Nevada, and Nancy had a solo. We came in third, and Nancy came in third out of a lot of schools — I forget how many schools there were. She was one of the really fortunate persons.

She was able to run for Homecoming Queen her senior year, and she won the election to be student body president. She was a leader. I mean she was a whole leader — making sure everyone was included and making sure that things are in its right place and that we have good spirit. I haven't been there for quite a while, but I don't think there has been ever a spirited year like it was in the 1978 and '79 school year at Red Bluff High. I never, ever have heard or seen at Red Bluff High such great leadership and commitment than what my older sister had. I was really lucky of her being ahead of me, because of really planting the seeds for me.

Nancy was a cheerleader. She also laid out the pathway for me by talking to sports people — football players and basketball players, etc.

I had three of her friends come up to me and say, "Anyone hassles you — giving you a rough time — you let me know, and I'll personally take care of it." They really did a lot of protecting and watching out for me.

Since I couldn't participate in sports, I wanted to be the equipment manager and water boy. That's how I got my mainstreaming in — besides PE. I was able to travel with the football team all throughout my years, and the basketball team, and the track team.

* * *

I really had a difficult time to be able to accept that I was going to be in special education with all people with disability. These were kids who lived at home and went to segregated sites for elementary and junior high; then they were mainstreamed on the campus at high school. By then that was the trend. I did not want to hang out with people in special education, except for during class periods where you're in the classroom — then you gotta be there with them. I did not want to associate with them outside of that.

I was the one that was in between cracks. I could hang out with people from sports in my freshman or sophomore year, because

Nancy laid the groundwork. So I acted kind of cruel to the other special education students, because I thought I was at a better level — I wasn't at their level. You know how society gets these cocky people they think they're better than everybody else. That's what I thought — I was the cheese in the special education courses, so I was cruel to them. I was very cruel, very cruel to people in special education in a situation of not hanging out with them, not wanting to be a part of their lives.

I hated it so much — the situation of a belief system that everyone that was non-disabled was looking at you as being different. You're mentally retarded. You're weird. You're not capable of associating with the high-popularity group.

And I always hated it, because inside the classrooms, I remember we had an alphabet up above the chalkboard. Here you are a freshman in high school, and you know the alphabet pretty much — you went through a public school system. They had pictures up on the wall, and these pictures were kind of degrading. What degrading means to me is where you are treated in a situation not at the level you think you are capable of being able to handle. Degrading also is where people see that you are getting put down. That rubs off to other people, so other people give you a harder difficult time to be able to achieve things.

They were pictures where you have a 'xample of three different apples, and you take one away, and that equals two. Pictures — drawn out — not like a photographer-type-of-situation. The artist draws it out, and you hang it up — pictures of more like pitiness — people being able to help other people. I don't like pictures where they just hang up on the wall because it's pity. Everyone loves them. To me, it's degrading having a picture up there, and when a person walks by, being able to look at the picture and saying, "Oh, ain't that cute. Somebody's helping somebody get in a wheelchair," or "Someone's helping with the cane."

Every Friday we had Game Day. I hated it! It was to be able to award us of the work that we did throughout the week. It was Game Day, so we played with cards and all of that kind of stuff. They thought it could help us with math and all this other stuff. I was always cruel in the situation of ... I didn't want to play. I did not want to play with a bunch of people with disabilities. I was much better than them; so I always had to end up doing something else — work on what I never got completed or start on next week's assignment.

Also, what I hated inside the classroom ... you always had this feeling that you were different. Even though you were right in the center of the campus, you were still different than everybody else. And I always remember walking down the hallway — always hearing people saying, "Don't walk down that hallway, because that's where the retards hang out."

It was a very isolated, frustrated, angry situation of always showing up to those classes in that territory. I also thought I was treated differently. I was a person who could not handle mainstreaming-type-of-situations because of my IQ and because of having a difficult time with books and comprehension and remembering things for tests and all of that. It was a feeling like you were in a prison. I haven't experienced what a prison is like, but it felt like a prison.

My parents thought this was the right decision for high school. They didn't think I would make it at all if I didn't go through special education.

However, I did have one teacher's aide — her name was Connie Spann. If it wasn't for her, I would've not been able to make it through high school. She was the one that really took the initiative to work with me on my requirements — making sure I will get through and graduate on time. That's the only person I really felt really comfortable around and wanted to be around all the time in the room.

* * *

In high school I wanted a lot of love and a lot of 'tention. I wanted that relationship like everybody else does — dating, and everything. One of the things I always did for the cheerleaders was to try and win one of them — to get involved with a relationship with a cheerleader. I always went out to buy birthday gifts. I think I had the intent of buying friendship. That was the way to be able to get a hug from 'em — get a kiss on the cheek. When there was a birthday, or when there was a ending sport and the cheerleaders were changing over to other cheerleaders, I always got 'em gifts ... as being able to say, "Thank you. I love you. I want to be a part of your life."

I wasted a lot of money. Where that money came from was the farm — working during the summer. Nancy and Kathy, all of us worked during the summer. Nancy went to a lot of cheerleading camps, also, so she had part of the summer off. Kathy went to basketball camps. But I worked all summer. My dad paid me for working, but instead of saving it up and investing it, I went out and spent it on women. That's how I thought I could get a relationship. That's how I thought I could date somebody. I find out, now, that no way you can do that. That doesn't do the trick.

* * *

I remember having a conversation with one of the special education teachers about what the word "retarded" means. He was a great teacher — he sat down and explained what it all meant. It happened one day after school. We got in a conversation and everything. He explained what it meant. That was the first time I ever really understood the words "mentally retardation." That made the belief system a lot stronger — that I was different — and the image of what the second-grade teacher said: "Your IQ is too low, and you're too mentally retarded ... " That's where it really got a lot stronger and really reinforces all the situation.

* * *

Not only I was in special education five periods out of six, one of the biggest barriers I faced in my high school was dating — being able to get involved in a relationship. Usually, when you're a sophomore and you turn sixteen, you're able to get your driver's license. Because of my disability, my family thought I shouldn't drive until I was about nineteen years old. So I didn't get that chance to really experience what everyone experiences — of being able to go to the dances, or to date somebody, go take 'em out to dinner, etc. One of the things I always ended up having to do was: If I went anywhere on a date, I always ended up having my mom or my father taking me. It wasn't always a thing where I could just go with my sister and double date, because they needed their time and their space. I did ask people, and I did go to homecoming dances, but my mother or father always ended up taking me and the date.

The barrier I faced was ... I was different. I had this label on me, and the label was that I was in special education. It was difficult for any woman to be able to want to date me. I remember I went to three of my homecoming dances. One of them bombed out. She saw somebody else there who she knows, and she rudely left me and stuck out with him the whole time. That was not a fun situation at all.

Then, I remember that I met this person in PE, and she always ended up waiting for me. She stood by the door, and she would not go into the class unless I showed up. No matter if she was late, she always would stay there wanting to go to class together and be my friend. Her name was Margarite.

I decided to ask her out, my sophomore year, to a Valentine's dance. She was excited that I asked her. We had to wait to let each other know if we could go. She was afraid to ask her parents. She didn't know if her parents would let her go. It was Thursday, and I heard from a friend that Margarite didn't want to go with me, and she didn't want to tell me that she didn't want to go with me. She didn't want to hurt my feelings — saying no to me. So she told this friend that she was just going to show up to the dance. I remember that really made me frustrated. It made me really upset. She was going to go — just show up to the dance by herself — and not let me know, because she didn't want to hurt me ... hurt my feelings.

I haven't heard a word from her, so I decided to go, and if I see her, I see her, and if I don't ... that's okay. I went to the dance and I saw her, and I said, "Margarite, how are you?"

She said, "Oh, I'm fine, Mike."

I said, "You want to dance?"

She said, "Yeah, I'll dance with you."

I said, "Margarite, what happened to you? I had plans of maybe going to dinner, and then to the dance, and have a fun time with you."

She said, "Mike, don't even start."

I said, "Well, lookit. You didn't let me know, and I don't think that's really fair in the situation."

She said, "Mike, my family's been sick all week. I didn't know that I was going to be able to come, so I didn't tell you anything."

I said, "At least you could have told me."

She said, "Mike, I'm feeling that you're getting angry, so let's split apart."

So what happened is that I sat down right by her, and she said, "Mike, I want to get one thing straight: I don't want a relationship with you. I don't want to hurt you. I'm your friend. I don't want a relationship with you."

I wanted to be able to have a relationship so much with her, because she was the perfect person to be able to share with. I loved her smile, and I loved her face, and I loved her personality, and I loved the way she met me at the door every time.

I got up, and I lifted my foot, and I slammed my foot down on the chair and busted the chair right in half. I said, "Fine! Be that way! I'll see you later."

We never talked for two and a half years. After my senior year, I saw her at a bowling alley. We sat down, and we talked it all out. It was incredible. We became best friends after high school, and we stayed in touch for a while.

CHAPTER FOUR

JUNIOR AND SENIOR YEARS

My first two years of high school, I didn't have any of the trouble that I did my last two years. But Nancy graduated when I was a sophomore, and I went into my junior year with Nancy already graduated. I really missed the people she knew.

It was my class that really put on the pressure of not accepting me as a person — who I really was. I had no idea of what was going to happen when they graduated — the junior and senior class. No idea at all.

I think the family got a lot closer because of the distance that Nancy went. We started missing having six kids upstairs. There's someone gone. They were still alive, but they were gone. I mean, physically, they were gone. Nancy was back in Indiana going to college ... back east in Anderson, Indiana. It was a four-year, private Christian school that she went to ... to major in music. Also, Becky went to Shasta College, and she was living in Redding.

I had a friend who worked for the school newspaper. She was one of the cheerleaders I knew because of sports — being equipment manager and all of that. Everyone knew Nancy, and Nancy graduated. My senior year I wrote in the school newspaper that this school was very dead — spiritually-wise. The spirit was gone. We did not have the spirit like we did in the late seventies — '78, '79. It's gone. What happened to it? Where's the leadership? It was a great big article. I criticized the whole school and everything. I really stuck my neck out; I always had a lot of guts. I got in trouble for it at home. I got grounded sticking my neck out too far.

My junior and senior year, I really fit more between the cracks, because I didn't want to hang out with people with developmental disability during my lunch or snack break, recess time, whatever. I couldn't really hang out with people from sports, because they didn't want to be a part of my life during my junior and senior year. I would say ... my junior and senior year I just had acquaintances. I wouldn't call the people on the teams my really true friends. I would call them just acquaintances. So that is really my experience with special education — how I feel about being in there.

No one really wanted me to be a part of the sports. Everyone treated me in the situation that I was different. I had to hang in there, because I loved sports. I wanted to be a part of sports.

My junior year I worked for the wrestling team. The rule was ... you're only supposed to get one towel, and I handed out towels after the practices. I hated this one wrestler. He was a cocky guy and I always loved his girlfriend, and I tried to steal her away from him. Yeah, she was a cheerleader. It didn't work out. So what happened one time, this guy I didn't like and another guy ... I wouldn't give them an extra towel. So they emptied a garbage can into another garbage can and then they filled that garbage can full of water. They came in and dumped it over my head. I was just drenched with water, so they grabbed two extra towels to get what they wanted. That was the price that I had to pay.

My senior year, we had a trip over to Reno, Nevada, for a high school game. I remember on the way over there all the players ...

what they did was really picked on me and harassed me. They hit me over the head with pillows trying to suffocate me. Then one of the ball players got kind of goofy and decided to light a lighter and hold the lighter up to my face.

He told me, "You don't belong on this earth. You're too retarded, and I want to burn you."

Instead of doing track my senior year, I was with the baseball team. They always harassed me also. Couple of people always harassed me in the situation of ... I was too mentally retarded to be able to be out with the people, and that mentally retarded people did not belong on the team.

I remember that we had a fund-raiser with the baseball team, and the fund-raiser was to play a hundred innings with another school. People would pitch in so much money for each inning that we would play. We'd get sponsors, and the money would go towards a new baseball field — a big diamond and new scoreboard. One of the things that I remember is someone stuck a sign on the back of me that I didn't even know was on me. It stayed on for about twenty innings, on my back.

I had a really close friend that came up to me and said, "Did you know that you have a sign on your back?"

I said, "No, I don't know I have a sign on the back."

He tored it off and gave it to me. What it was reading was, "You're mentally retarded. Why are you on this team?"

It was a parent out in the audience that came up to me and told me. I remember, also, the baseball team situation where no one wanted me to be able to travel, and they always tried to talk the coach out of having me travel with the team.

Bottom line: It's just a lack of education. I think it's the parents who don't have awareness of people with developmental disabilities. Kids — they're always willing to learn, but it's the parents who hold them back from learning about other people.

I think this goes back to the sixties — with the KKK groups and all of that down in the South. I mean, it's the same type of ignorance — not understanding. We had a pretty scary, frightening thing that happened about sixty miles out of Sacramento in a little town called Modesto. The KKK got all together and burned the cross. That said they're alive and ready to take on the world again; so it's still around.

I think education and training is the answer of everything in the world ... and role models. People that have developmental disabilities need to go back and be responsible to go put on the training. That's why I really want to put all this money — of my share that I get from this book — into a trust. And one of the biggest things I want to be able to do is put on disability awareness — hire people to be able to do disability awareness and hire consumers. That's my main goal.

* * *

I was taking math and reading, and I was taking social studies — all of the classes that were required by the State of California in special education. I had to have 280 units to be able to graduate from Red Bluff High — that was the minimum requirement for the State of California back in those years. Special education teachers would teach the whole class, but then also, we divided up into little different groups. We started out as a large group; then we divided up into smaller groups. That's where the aides helped to be able to help us understand all of the stuff. That's how I would graduate — take all the courses through special education, and then I could say I passed high school and get the real diploma.

My junior year there was a law passed that people in high school had to pass this reading and math and English proficiency test — on top of the 280 units. If you didn't past this proficiency test, you wouldn't graduate; you wouldn't get your diploma. I had a principal that told me this in the fall semester of my junior year. He knew that my parents would be right up there knocking on the door if he gave me special treatment of this — being able to not take the test and being able to create a special waiver-type-of-situation, because I was in special education.

He said, "I don't know what we're going to be able to do to help you to get through this, but I want you to know I'm committed to finding out a way to have you get through this test."

It was only given once a year; so that means I only had two times to be able to pass it. I took it during the fall of my junior year, and I didn't pass it. In the spring of my junior year I got called in, and the principal said, "I got good news for you."

I said, "What's that?"

And he said, "We're going to have a summer class for people who didn't pass it during the school year — to be able to take a six-week course and be able to go ahead and pass it during the summer, giving you another opportunity."

During that conversation I said, "You gotta make me a promise."

He said, "What's that?"

"Make sure the air conditioners work."

It was incredible. I took four hours of summer school each day for about eight weeks out of the twelve weeks that we had off. The air conditioners worked, so it was pretty cool. I was ready to take the test at the end of the six weeks, and I passed it. So I was able to graduate — if I got the 280 units on time in the four years.

* * *

My senior year, I got so tired of PE being the only class I was mainstreamed in. I wanted to be able to get into another class where there were no other special education students. I wanted to be like I was kindergarten through eighth grade — in the general mainstream, in the general education course.

I talked a little bit about it to Mom and Dad, but they never really pushed any buttons or anything. They think that I would have a very difficult time of passing the course. They had the same belief as the counselor and special education people did — that I was uncapable of probably succeeding.

Now, I remember I went to my counselor and said, "I want to be able to take a course."

She didn't exactly say it, but I knew what she meant — that I was not capable of taking a general education course. That I had a hard time with reading and comprehension and being able to understand what's going on in the classroom.

I said, "I want to be in another class where there're general education students and a general education teacher."

It was amazing that she said, "Well, let's think about it. We'll make an appointment, and we'll call the special education teachers into this meeting that we'll have, and we'll talk about it. Meanwhile, why don't you go talk to your special education teacher and see if he thinks it's a good idea?"

I talked to my teacher, and he didn't think I would be able to handle the course. He said — about my comprehension level — that I would not be able to be a part of the class and participate in the class. It would not be able to work out. It would not be feasible.

He said, "You're getting a real diploma. Why do you want to mess that up? The only thing that you're missing is civics government, and we can take that course in here. It's a lot more easier book than it is up there in the general education situation."

I said, "I want you in the meeting next week ... to be able to go over this with the counselor. I want to get into a class."

He said that it was impossible and there was no way I should do it. But he did it anyway. He went in, and I went in, and the counselor went, and we talked about it. He said that it would be not a good situation; then the counselor said that she thought of an idea that maybe I could go in the class that is a semester long. I could take it during the fall semester, and if I fail it, I would have a head start of everybody else, and I can retake it during the spring. She said that way I would have a head start and everything.

I said, "No. I don't want to do it that way. I want to challenge myself. Let me take it during the spring semester."

So what happened is — it was amazing — there was a teacher that teaches civics that decided to take me in the spring semester. There were nine people that didn't have any disabilities at all who failed the course during the fall. Basically, why I think they failed is because they didn't care and they didn't do the homework. These nine people got told that there was a person in special education with a developmental disability that was going to come in and be in this class. They got to be able to treat him as an equal — like everybody treats everybody else.

The teacher told them that, not only that you got to treat him as an equal, but you got to be able to do homework with him, and you got to be able to inter-react with him and be a part of his life. He said it right in the middle of everybody when I came into the classroom.

Then the teacher said, "If you do this, you and I will not have any trouble. If you don't do it, you and I will have trouble."

That teacher was Chris Bauer, a very athletic guy, very tall — six-foot-nine, six-foot-eight, somewhere around there. Very athletic. He coached basketball before I became a freshman. Just genuine, down-to-earth. His classroom was a room of humbleness, a class that you always want to show up to because of the environment in there and everything. He had control of his class. He was a very honest man — very dedicated to help others out.

It was amazing. I was in this general education class that was civics government where people were non-disabled, and the teacher was a general education teacher. And it was exciting that we were gonna team up in teams. There were three different groups — two groups had three, and the one group of four. I was in the group of four.

One of the assignments was that we had to be able to think how to make a bill, and how to be able to pass that bill, and how to testify for that bill. The ground rules were that if you pick up a topic, and you didn't find anything in the library on that topic, you had to make it up. You can't change your topic. You can't change it at all. So when we got to go off into the library and we dig up all these books, we researched it. The topic that we put in our group was motorcycle helmets: There must be a law for motorcycle helmets, and why.

There was no information at all in the library about motorcycle helmets, so we had to start from scratch. We couldn't change the subject matter; we had to stay with motorcycle helmets. So we got together and we brainstormed. What is a motorcycle helmet? What are motorcycles? Why should you wear motorcycle helmets? What would be the purpose of saving lives?

We had about two weeks to do this assignment. After the two weeks was up, we formed a Senate and an Assembly. Then you would have to testify to those people, and then they would vote on the situation of … Should a bill like this pass? The governor was the teacher, and he would have the final sign-off of the bill.

One of the things that was so amazing about the whole situation was we got up there, and we testified by taking different parts. I testified on why should people wear helmets. It was just totally incredible — standing in front of and being able to testify in front of everybody, and being a part of the real-society situation. Our bill passed by one vote, and the teacher signed off on it, so it became law. The amazing thing about this whole situation ... about eight years later, someone did sponsor a bill in California to wear motorcycle helmets, and it passed.

The other exciting thing was I was able to study for tests and finals with individuals in my group and in the class and being able to be a part of a class. It was just amazing, through the semester, how much I saw things, and how much I achieved, and how much support — natural support — that I got through the teacher.

Everyone thought that there was an earthquake happen in Red Bluff, but there really wasn't. What the earthquake was ... I sent shockwaves through the administration saying that I can't take a course like that, and I got a B+ out of the course. That was the earthquake.

If it wasn't for that individual teacher, I would not be sitting here today, developing this story. That teacher had such a impact on my whole life. I think how he changed my life is ... taking the chance of being able to have me in his class and all the stuff that I learned from him. It just made me such a better person. It taught me how to be on the Board of Directors, and how a city council is run and how the government is run. This Chris Bauer, he really done a number for me ... giving me more empowerment — tools to work with later on in life — than any teacher out of thirteen years of public education.

* * *

At the end of my senior year, I had a IEP meeting. That's Individual Education Plan where all the teachers get together — special education teachers — and develop a plan of action: strengths, weaknesses, and all of that. Then you have quarterly meetings on that. I had that done all through my high school years. We were outnumbered by administrators — the psychologist, special education teachers, executive director, assistant executive director, and the principal. That's the problem with today's special education for parents — they're outnumbered by bureaucrats!

So we had this IEP meeting, and Chris Bauer was invited. The question came up, "What do you see Michael being capable of doing in the future?" He was the last one being asked in the room about that. Everyone else went before him — my family, special education teachers, principal, psychologist — everyone answered.

One of the things that was said all throughout the meeting was, "Michael's capable of getting a job like at a newspaper or at a fast-food place or a janitorial position — as a janitor at the hospital. We can see him doing a lot of things with people, because that's what he likes — people. That's his quality — people. We don't see Michael capable of going on to college and getting a degree."

It was amazing. When Chris had his time to share, he said, "I have bigger dreams for Michael than what all you have in this room. I see Michael with potential far more than whatever you guys see. How does he get there? I don't know. That's the problem that his family is going to face, and other people are going to face. But he's much more capable than working on a farm, much more capable than working at some fast-food restaurant, much more capable than as a janitor, much more capable of doing what you all say."

Chris was the only one that went beyond anybody, saying, "You're just selling Michael short of all his capabilities that he does have."

That kind of gave me confidence in the situation that I'm a capable and willing man. But no one really came up with any decision. It was kind of left open to my family and I what I want to do. So there was really no follow-up. I think that's what's really sad — parents have people with developmental disabilities and give 'em to the schools for twenty-two years, or nineteen years, or eighteen years, and then, wow. What's next? They got babysit, basically, all their lives.

That's why I really like the transition stage of beginning working now in high school. There's a program in California where they transition them in employment at a sophomore level, so they start getting work experience and start building their resume.

I came up four years short, my teacher said. He said I came up four years short of all the transition working. I've always went back to see my teachers; I always went and visit the campus and see my special education teachers. I had three of them, and Chris Bauer.

* * *

We had a track meet in Oroville, which is about an hour and a half southeast of Red Bluff. I was the equipment manager for the track team, and after the track meet our bus broke down on the way home in between Oroville and Chico. I had to get home, because my sister was singing in a wedding and I wanted to see the wedding. There was this school bus that came right behind us. It was a school from Redding, and they offered to take all the women off our bus and drop 'em off at the high school because

Red Bluff came before Redding did.

I said, "Coach, Coach! I need to go! I need to go with those women! They need to find room for one more person."

I just had this incredible gut feeling that I was going to meet somebody on this bus. I just had this weird feeling.

I said, "Coach, remember, I gotta be back for this wedding!" I knew that this wedding was all over with.

So I got on the bus and everyone booed me, because it was jam-packed. I mean, there was like two people to a seat and some three to a seat. I sat down in one of the seats that had two people. There was this woman from the Redding school that was called Enterprise that said, "I don't want you to sit there!"

I said, "But there's no room."

"I don't care. I don't want you to sit there."

Across the aisle, this girl scooted over and she said, "You can sit here."

We talked all the way home. We met each other, and I was in love with this girl. Her name was Chasity. Oh, finally! At last! I'm going to be able to get a girlfriend! I was going to be able to get to see somebody, even though that she lived thirty miles away. We ended up 'changing addresses when we got home in Red Bluff, and I was just so fired up. I can have Mom take me up there, or she can come down and see me, because she had her driver's license. I was just ... oh ... I was psyched!

This was my sophomore year. I called her all the time, and she came down and saw me. We just had a really good friendship, and it was working into a relationship-type-of-situation.

Then my senior year I was able to ask her to the homecoming dance. I was really amazed that she said yes, because I didn't even know that the same night was her homecoming night, and she didn't say anything about it. It meant a lot to me that she would give up her homecoming dance to come to my dance. She went out to dinner with me and to the football game, and she had to sit with some of my sisters and family, because I was out on the football field being equipment manager.

I was so fired up I could not believe it. We got to dance and we had a blast.

She said, "Michael, I want to tell you something ... I want to be able to just be your friend. I don't want a relationship. I don't want to hurt you. If we dated seriously, I would hurt you, and I don't want to do that."

So again, I thought I had an opportunity to be able to date someone and get serious, but then, again the label came up and controlled the whole situation: I was in special education, and no one wanted to be able to hurt me. I was different. I was not the same. I couldn't handle a relationship.

* * *

My dad and mom were very involved with the church. I remember every Easter morning we had the youth groups out at our house for a big pancake breakfast after sunrise service. That was the fun days of being able to be a part of that. Mom and Dad always threw parties. In fact, the last seven years, Mom and Dad always had the church out on Tuesday nights June through July. Every Tuesday night they have barbecue swim parties.

Mom and Dad sold one of the orchards to pay off another orchard, and then we had enough money left for making a decision of a ski boat or a swimming pool. It was a tie of what the family wanted. Dad didn't want no ski boat! Dad didn't want to haul it around; so we got a swimming pool. The parties were not only that, but ... you know how some of the times high school graduations you have the big keg party, and all of that kind of stuff? You know? Everyone go out and get drunk and celebrate? Well, Mom and Dad always believed that kids shouldn't drink. So we always had a graduation swimming party all night long after graduation — all the way up until eight o'clock the next morning. Somewhere the kids could go who didn't drink and didn't want to drink. We always had about two, three hundred people out there celebrating and just having a blast. We did that for many, many years.

Graduation was a really incredible, emotional night. I didn't know what was going on. They had this white carpet rolled out in front of the podium on the edge of where the class is sitting. The counselor introduced the names of the graduates, and the principal and the Chairperson of the Board of Directors were at the end of this white carpet. The end of it is the middle of the two sections of the class. Over to the right side, which was on the north side, was the football bleachers, where all family members and friends sat.

When our row got up and we walked around, I got right up front to that white carpet. The counselor called my name out, and I didn't want to look to the south where the class was sitting. Didn't want to look to the north where all the family members were looking. I just got on the white carpet and started walking down, and my head was down. All of the sudden, I got this urge to lift my head up, look over to the left — that's to the south — and all the classmates stood up and started clapping. I think it was for me — that I made it through, that I accomplished what everyone else does.

Then I got this urge to look over to the right, which is the north part of the bleachers. They stood up and started clapping. I was just overwhelmed with all this cheering, and I put my head right back down. I got to the end of the carpet, and I reached my right hand out to shake the principal's hand, and my left hand I stuck underneath the right arm and grabbed — not heavy grabbed, but I gently grabbed — the diploma out of the Board of Director Chairman's hand and shake the principal's hand. Then I put my head back down, and I walked toward my seat, and I sat down. I didn't look straight out; I looked down. I put my arms on my knee, and my head was kind of bowed. I was looking straight down to the ground.

And that was it. That was graduation. Five seconds of walking down a white carpet.

After putting up with all of the baloney that I put up with for thirteen and a half years, or fourteen years, it came to end. So I had to sit through all the rest of 'em. I started going out and looking for a friend, 'cause we threw up our hats, and we had a class song, and we started out looking for friends.

I couldn't find anybody. I was like a lost sheep in this great herd of sheeps. I couldn't find anybody or anything; I was confused. I ran up to the north side of the bleachers to go try to find somebody; I ran back down to the football field. I couldn't find anybody. Then twenty minutes later, I ran into the two best people in my whole life — that was my mother and my father that was supporting me all the way.

They said, "Congratulations, Mike. You made it through."

They reached out and gave me a great big hug. One of the things that I said was, "Mom, Dad, twelve and a half years sucked big-time. I only enjoyed one semester of thirteen years of public education, and that was the class that I had in civics my senior year."

They said, "We're sorry."

And that was graduation.

CHAPTER FIVE

WORKING ON THE FARM

So we had to make some decision what was next for Michael. A lot of the people that were on the football team and basketball teams went to junior colleges and then went to universities also. Some of them went to work. Everyone had their different planning strategy. I felt really angry and upset that I couldn't handle going to a college. I never got to experience the college experience that ninety percent of Americans do experience, and I missed it. That's where my world was kind of isolated. It was a world of completely segregation. I did have family friends, but most of my family friends were adult — family friends of my mom and dad. That was a lot of fun to be able to have, but no one really was the same age as I was. So that was a really difficult transition period for myself.

I did go to this junior college in Redding, about a half an hour north of Red Bluff — Shasta Junior College. Sometimes I took the bus up there, and sometimes I got rides from other people from Red Bluff who I knew. They were out of my sister, Nancy's, class. Also, there was a couple other people who helped me — that was on the junior college football team — who lived in Red Bluff. They gave me rides back, also.

It wasn't really all farm country. It was really bare high-grass area all the time. It was brown and ugly, because it was all dried out, basically. But the college was kind of like in the foothills of

Redding, and the campus was really beautiful because of the landscaping. They really made an effort to be able to keep up the landscaping ... keep everything green. It was a very beautiful, beautiful campus. Of course, I always loved to watch all the women walk around on campus, also.

I thought it was going to be a big successful-type-of-situation. I was really looking forward to doing that — helping out with the athletic department. But the semester just did not work.

Junior college was courses of beginning math and beginning reading — really like special education courses that I signed up for. It was no class of science or any of that kind of stuff. I just wanted to help out the football team, and that was the way to be able to do it. I got to work with the football team, to be equipment manager for the football team, and that was a lot of fun. I got to travel a lot with the football team to different cities, and that was a lot of fun, too.

But college was not the thing for me. I tried out a semester of it, and I came to the decision — I don't know how — that I wasn't succeeding, and I need to go out and look for a job. I didn't know what I wanted to do.

My next step was I looked at jobs in Red Bluff. The type of jobs that I was looking for was inventory in the sports department, dishwasher at a restaurant. I remember when I went for interviews, I couldn't be able to get things down correctly. They knew something was different about this person. *Cognitively, he's not here. Cognitively, he's out in left field. He won't be a good worker for us. He can't do the job.* Everyone who I interviewed with and filled out a application and turned it in — everyone knew I was different than the average person. They didn't always say that Michael was not the one to be able to fit the job. They didn't say

... because of his disability. They would say, "Because you're not strong enough in this area," or, "We're looking for a specific type of situation."

Those type of jobs were fast-food jobs — working as dishwashers and janitors ... what everyone wanted me to do at the IEP meetings. So nobody wanted to hire me. I wasn't successful anywhere. I didn't get hired anywhere.

I end up working for my dad. I hated it. I *hated* it. I didn't like it at all. I worked for him for two years, I think it was. What I did is stuff that I had been doing during the summers.

From August through November, that's harvest season. From December through March is when they do a lot of pruning for new growth to come on trees — a lot of piled brush and things. From March through July is when they do a lot of irrigation. It's like another harvest — between March and July. What I mean by that is you got a lot of things to do, not only irrigation; so you're always on the go. In between the irrigation, we always keep the grass low and always mow the grass by a tractor. We got this thing on a hook on the tractor that's called a chopper. The chopper has teeth, and it rolls and makes the teeth go around and round to mow your grass. Why you always want to have low grass is because, for harvest, when the shaker comes and shakes the nuts down, you want to be able to have the sweeper to come along and blow all the nuts into a windrow.

In high school years, I learned how to run the tractor. Greg was doing it since he was a kid. I 'ventually wanted to be tried out. One of the things that I always had trouble with ... I always ended up running into the trees and scraping the trees, and the trees would die. My father never believed in what we call strip spraying. Strip spray is where you kill about two feet from the tree outward — all the grass in between that two feet of length. He never believed in that, because of the expense that it would cost. Where I had trouble — running into trees — is not to be able to have that two feet, that cushion where I won't bump into the tree. The chopper — the mower — was about ten feet long hooked on the back of the tractor. There was about a foot and a half stick out a little farther to the right. It's not centered — like where you have five feet on both sides; one side is about eight feet long. That's the best way I could explain it. Without that two feet, I always end up bumping the trees and skinning the trees.

Another problem was when we put out the irrigation pipe. We have a pipe trailer where all the pipe is on this trailer pulled by this tractor. You gotta be careful about not turning a corner too sharply; then the tree would hit the pipe, and then it would bust the pipe off, or it would mash the pipe, or it would bend it where it won't hook into the pipe where it's supposed to hook into. So it was always a struggle for me to be able to get around corners, and I bent up a lot of pipe.

I always got chewed out by my father. He did it in a loving way, but he was doing it like any other boss would probably do it. I think he was a little harder on me, because he had a harder time to accept me, I believe. Not only that he had a harder time to accept me, he was harder on me because I was a family member. You never want to work for your family, because they expect 5,000 times more out of you than what they do in the situation of a regular employee; so it's really difficult. I had a lot of low self-esteem. I always was nervous about hitting a tree, or bending up a pipe, or doing something ...

My father had to make a management decision ... and when you go out and skin up all the trees — when they die — you're not going to have any crops, so ...

He said, "You're going to have to be the one on the back and put pipe out."

The last year of the three years that I worked there, I always ended up not driving the tractor. We did the switching around to find the right place for me — to accommodate the situation of not causing any damage to trees or not causing any damage to pipe. I always ended up pulling off the pipe and then lay it on the ground.

I always had a hard time coordinating things with equipment. I really never ran any equipment. It was a lot of changing pipe, a lot of putting out irrigation pipe and stuff. Other people really drove.

One of the things that also was difficult for me was keeping up with the other guy in front of me, because it takes two guys to lay pipe out. Each pipe's about thirty feet long, and you have a main line, then you have a valve. The main lines hook up to a pump, and the water comes down that main. You open the valve, and then it just shoots all the way down to your end of your sprinklers, and the sprinklers irrigate the orchards. What happens is: When you lay the pipe out, you gotta be able to have two people — one in front and one in back — and be able to hook it up all the time.

I always had a hard time keeping up with the hired workmen, because they have more coordination, more speed, more all those different things that I really didn't have; so it was really frustrating. Also, when we changed irrigation pipe from one valve to the next valve, there were three other people, and I was still on the first row when they got four rows done. They did three times as much as work as I did. That was always frustrating.

A lot of Americans really would not want to work in the farm area, so Mom and Dad always hired, legally, people from Mexico — Spanish people that came from Mexico for a better life to live. All of these people who worked for us always saved their money up and sent it back to Mexico for their families. They leaved their families back there sometimes; sometimes they'd bring 'em up. There wasn't no ghetto type of thing in Red Bluff because all the farmers always had trailers or houses on their property.

That's what's so nice about the whole situation — there isn't that ghetto in one specific area of town. Most of them really kept everything up nice and neat. We never had, that I remember, any trouble of having people be messy. Always everything is nice and neat and tidy.

Basically, I did not relate to any of the workers on the farm. When we were out changing irrigation pipe, they already got their rows down while I was still working. I got about three-fourths of my row done when they already got their row done; so they always came over to help me finish up. That created barriers between me and the co-workers. It was a really low self-esteem situation. Also, I think there was nobody to really share your feelings with. When you were out changing irrigation pipes, there was no really communication in between each orchard that you had to go and change — in between where you had to ride. That wasn't because of the barrier between Spanish and English, because all of the Spanish people were able to talk English as a second language. They could understand. It was a barrier of ... I was different. I was much lower. So people really frowned on that situation.

The type of job that I really loved was riding on the tractor and be able to chop the grass or mow the grass. Because I had my own speed, no one else was around or anything like that. But when you go out, and skin up all the trees ...

It was a lot of hard physical work during June through August. The temperature was usually over a hundred, and sometimes it was up in the high hundreds — 117 and 118.

* * *

My father didn't believe that I would go very far in life because of my cognitive skills. But he was a man that did not want me to go on welfare — Social Security and SSI and disability. What they dreamed about is I would live right down the street from them. They dreamed that I would have a job, and when they go on vacation, I'll go on vacation with them. If I don't want to go on vacation with them, I would only just go see my sisters or my brother. I would not have the variety of choice of going outside the boundaries of California. I was not capable of doing that, because people spot other people who are slower or who have a more difficult time. They take advantage of people. That was the biggest concern that my family had: They don't want Michael to be taken advantage of. I could see it because of the sheltered environment I lived in.

As I was growing up, I seen everyone else do a lot of other things, and I didn't do those things. Like in seventh and eighth grade, they have parties at somebody's house — birthday parties or slumber parties. A lot of people went, and I didn't go.

My parents tried to include me in a lot of the church things; that's where I really was not in the shelter environment. I was really included with a lot of the youth group activities and junior high activities as the church does, and I'm really grateful for that. At the church groups, they didn't pick on me. But it was hard for me to fit in, because they knew I had a much slower time in doing things and comprehending things and being able to be a part of a conversation.

I participated in 4-H, too. But I hated 4-H. It wasn't the thing for me. One of the things about 4-H ... here again it was, *Michael is different, and he has a much harder time.* So people always liked to harass me and give me a hard time ... like Boy Scouts and all the fun things that kids have an opportunity to be a part of. They harassed and teased and lacked understanding of people who are different.

I wasn't dating at all because I didn't have my driver's license. Chasity — the gal that I met her when I was a freshman in high school — the problem with her was she was more of a sister. I wanted more than a sister-relationship. I wanted *the* relationship.

CHAPTER SIX

THE BAY AREA

One day I ended up saying, "Dad, I want to talk to you." He said, "Well, talk."

I said, "Well, let's go for a ride."

So we went for a ride, and I said, "Dad, I want to tell you … I know this ain't probably very good … but I'm giving my notice today and I'm leaving tomorrow."

He said, "What do you mean?"

I said, "Dad, I want to tell you that I'm moving down to San Francisco. Our friend Robert is going to let me stay there until I've found a job."

Robert was a family friend; my mother went to school with Robert's father. Robert was three years older than I was, and we were staying in touch. We were friends, and he lived on the peninsula of the Bay Area — San Carlos was the neighborhood. It was both of our ideas. We were talking about it for months, and he checked it out with the people who he was living with. He was going to stay there, and I would come down and live there also. He would go to college while I would go to work.

Dad said, "You sure you want to do this?"

I said, "Yeah, I'm sure I want to do this."

He said, "Well. You got a place to live, but what about work?"

I said, "Dad, I'm going to get a job. I got a reference, and it's you. I'm working for you quite a while now."

THE BAY AREA

He said, "You really want to do this?"

I said, "Yeah, Dad. I want to be able to ask you another thing. Please, comfort Mom."

He said, "Well, what do you mean by comforting Mom? Something going to happen to you?"

I said, "No, Dad. This is our strategy: I'm packing my suitcases while she's in town, and Bob is going to be here before she gets back. We're loading the suitcases up, and we're out of here before she gets back. I'm not going to be able to say goodbye."

He said, "Man, you really make it difficult for me, don't you?"

I said, "Yeah, Dad. I'm sorry. I really want to be able to do this, though. You know she won't let me go."

Where we headed off to was the Bay Area — San Francisco, the Peninsula. I avoided the phone all that night when I got there, because I know … There were all these messages: "Please, call home." So I avoided the situation. I had a meeting with somebody the next morning.

Finally, Monday I called. I said, "Mom, I got a job!"

"Michael, you never do this again!"

"Mom, I got a job!"

"Michael, you never do this again!"

She said, "Where are you? What are you doing? What's going on?"

I said, "Mom, I got a job in San Carlos!"

"Where's San Carlos?"

I said, "It's the Bay Area."

She said, "Well … okay. Good. You got a job. Never do this again!"

She was overprotective, but she has this side on her that I never saw until I got out of the house. She backed off and became more of a friend. Very giving. Very, very loving. Supportive. She's seen what I've been able to do.

So the people Robert was living with knew this youth minister. I had a meeting with him, and he said he had a friend that owned a veterinarian hospital who had a position opening up — kennel work, and inventory and stocking, and helping take X-rays of animals. So he called him up, and he met us for lunch. By the end of the lunch he said, "You ready to work Monday morning at seven o'clock?"

I said, "Yes, let's go for it."

So I was there at seven o'clock.

I moved on Wednesday, and Thursday I met this minister. Friday we met this veterinarian for lunch, and Monday I started the job. I worked there for two years.

* * *

Out of that whole family, Robert and I were the only close ones. I don't know why that is, but we stay in contact up to today.

Bob never gave me a bad time; he's always been close. He kinda liked to pick on me — a different pick on, not make fun of. It's playing jokes, like everybody does. It's a natural, human joking-type-of-pick-on-ness that he plays.

Mom and Dad really worried about Bob and me being in the wrong place at the wrong time, but that never happened at all. Bob showed my parents where he has really stuck up for me and went out of his way in being my friend — supporting me in all the things that I have done and wanted to achieve.

Robert went to college. The elderly couple he lived with met me. I took care of their back yard during the weekends and at night. I was at work during the day. I had so much fun taking care of their back yard for 'em. They had a swimming pool, and so we got to go swimming. It was a beautiful place — just a really beautiful house. It was one story, and it had five bedrooms.

The people were awesome. She had multiple sclerosis, so she always had people working for them because she used a wheelchair. She had a bunch of attendants — in-home supports. Instead of rest homes, they decided to keep her at home. He owned this big business. He was a wholesaler between farmers and grocery stores — a middleman of getting all the vegetables for markets. He was a really successful businessman. They had five kids — beautiful, beautiful kids: three daughters and two boys. They were all gone. All of them were married, very successful in their marriage and very successful in life. They all have kids, so all the grandkids come over on the weekend to play with Grandma and Grandpa. They made sure we were included. We ate with the family. It was more a family-setting atmosphere there — a really family atmosphere.

It was just great, I mean, just a really great family life situation. I can't remember if Robert was related or how he got connected up with them, but he did tell me about it. He said, "You gotta come down here and experience this." So that's how I did it.

* * *

The only friends that I really had during that time was my family and the people we were staying with. Someone at the Regional Center introduced me to this person by the name of Ruth. We went out a couple of times, but I didn't have really any social life.

I found out down there about the Regional Center through a friend at work. The Regional Centers provide services for people with developmental disabilities in California. I wanted to see if I qualify for services ... and I did. I didn't have anything scheduled in the morning hours, and it was basically the morning-hours situation.

The kind of services I was getting was independent living training: how to keep a checkbook, how to do cooking, how to be able to make different recipes, how to problem-solve situations, if I got in a jam situation (which I always ended up doing in Chico later on). So that's how I got services. Those were the kind of services I got.

The veterinarian's hospital was so great. I never thought that I would really like the position at all. But it was so much fun because I got to take X-rays. If all my inventory was done and all the kennels were all cleaned up, I got to go in and watch surgery and be a part of surgery. I had tools and I knew the different parts of the tools. It was a lot of fun also, because a lot of the famous football players had pets, and that was their veterinary place.

There was a guy right next door to the veterinarian place where he owned his own grooming place to groom cats and dogs. He was just a character. I mean ... he was an old guy, in his sixties or seventies, and he loved to harass the people over in the veterinarian hospital. I got a lot of teasing from him. It was a big difference from high school. For one thing, it was more joking in the situation of playing tricks ... of hiding things on me ... than words. Words are more damaging; so it was more of a friendship teasing and I'd tease him back. It was a two-way street. I knew that he'd really go out of the way for me.

The hospital was right in the middle of Redwood City in a commercial area. Right down the street there was a big shopping center. One of the things that I didn't like about my job is that I

THE BAY AREA

always hated to go down to that Lucky store and pick up a bunch of tampons for the cats. What they used 'em for was for blood — if cats were bleeding, or in heat, or for operations. I didn't like buying those things ... and baby food. One of the things that cats do if they're in there, they eat baby food. It's easier. That was one of the biggest things that I bought — baby food. I don't know why they eat baby food, but one of the main ingredients that they get was baby food.

I took a city bus to work. It was on one of the main drags. I was a city boy! I loved it. I loved every minute of it. I was so excited. I hated the country. I get to go to professional baseball games. I always saved money for that. I'd been in San Francisco in the past; my grandma always took me to the games. I usually took the bus. They have city buses that go to the games. Robert helped me with the bus system. So I was this big-shot city person, and I really loved it. I had a vision that that was what I wanted to do for my whole life — stay at the veterinarian's hospital.

One time I walked in to work, and I heard this funny noise ... kind of like a waterfall that you would hear. When I got in the back, it was the water pipe that broke. Water was all over the place — about three to four inches high, all the way 'round. So I called my supervisor and told him. He came down and shut the thing off, and we mopped up everything and got everything all cleaned up.

A week later I came in and ... it was scary that time. I saw all this stuff scattered all over the place, glass all over the floor, a phone off the hook. I said, "Something's not right here." Then I walked in the back, and I saw a window busted.

I said, "Oh, we got burglarized. Someone broke into this place. What am I supposed to do? I don't want to call 911; I'll probably be stuck being responsible."

So I called my supervisor ... to be able to call 911 for me. I had to talk to the investigator anyway, 'cause I was the first one in the building. That made me look like the one who broke into this animal hospital. I can't remember if anything was taken, but I know there was glass on the floor, and I didn't want to get involved with it.

I didn't work any nighttime hours. At night I usually went out with people from the youth group that I was involved with at the church. I also went out with people from work. We always got together once a week and went out and have happy hour and shoot the breeze. I always had a soda to drink. One of the persons at work lived in an apartment right on the ocean, so I always asked to be able to get a ride over there. Other times I went up to the ocean and just walk on the beach.

I loved it. It was incredible. There could be one thing that I didn't like, and that was the cost of it ... the cost of living there, even though that I had pretty cheap rent — a hundred dollars a month.

* * *

It was in the Bay Area when I registered to vote the first time. I was twenty-two years old. At that time, it was Ronald Reagan for president, and Mondale. They had the Democratic Convention in San Francisco when I lived there, and I got to see Mondale walking up to his hotel.

That was when I got my license — was the last year. I was like twenty-one, twenty-two years old, and I decided to get my driver's license. My parents did not want me to have my license at sixteen, because of liability. After I turned eighteen, I was American, independent, adult-situation, so the whole liability went off. The liability was up to me. Still, at that time, I didn't feel confident enough to be able to get my license. And then at the age of twenty-one, I did get my license.

I had a friend at work help me to be able to do that — read the booklet and stuff. I got my permit, and Robert went out and helped me drive around for six months. I went and take the DMV test, and I passed the test. I got a station wagon car from my family. Within the first six months of my driving, I got into several automobile accidents — some of them were fender-benders. I was not hurt in none of them. The Bay Area was a really difficult area to be able to get around and move around. There's a lot of traffic and a lot of responsibility. I think another thing is that I was still a kid — not being a mature driver — which caused those accidents. One of them ... I did not see a stop sign where it was blocked, and they did not have the word "Stop" sprayed out on the road. After that, I dropped the driving.

* * *

My father came down and surprised me one night, when I was about twenty-four years old. He met me at work. He came down to see me and check up on me. If I remember correctly, the reason why he also came down is ... he had a meeting down in the Bay Area to go to. He decided to make extra time to be able to stop by and see how I was doing and share an evening together. He met me at work.

He said, "I want to go out to dinner with you."

I said, "Okay. I'll finish up in about ten minutes."

We went out to dinner. He said, "Mike, I 'member what you were saying at graduation night ... that you didn't like your school, and it was difficult for you. I know it was really difficult, but I couldn't be able to handle to put you in a segregated school, because of what other people would think of me."

I think Dad didn't want it to be hard on me — that I'm different, that he had a son that was different. He didn't want it to affect his friends, if they noticed that I wasn't part of the main, general education school.

So we had dinner and that's when he started opening up about the past and everything. It just happened. Then we went out for a drive after we ate. It was great when we were driving around and driving back to dropping me off where I was living at the time.

He and Mom ... they were really amazed of how well I was doing. Dad was telling me how he's really proud of me getting a job, and that he was really proud with the situation of how things really have went really well. We just got talking about everything.

Then he said, "Mike, I thought we did the best that we could ever do."

He wanted to make sure that I didn't have any anger towards Mom and himself. He knew that it was very difficult for me to handle situations of being harassed and being teased and being different. And so he was clearing the airway — developing a father-son relationship, basically.

I told him it was the best thing. I said, "Dad, you know you did the best that you could do. You thought that what you did was right. It's all over and done with, and we can't do nothing about it now."

I said, "You know, if I had a chance to relive my life again, I probably would want to go through the same thing as I did all of those years."

He said, "Why would you want to do that?"

I said, "Well, Dad, it taught me a lot of things — made me grow. Made me fight. Made me get this job here on my own ... showing that I can get a job and being able to be productive. Yes, it's inventory; and yes, it's cleaning up kennels; and yes, it's helping out on X-rays. But I love it. It's fun. I enjoy going to work day in and day out every day, and you guys literally helped me get to this place. All that harassing and trouble I went through in school — that's what helped me get here. You know what? I want to tell you something, Dad. Might have taken me twenty-three years to be able to get where I'm at — of having this job for a couple of years, but that's okay. It took that. What's important to be able to recognize is that I've made it on my own."

It's nutrition — going through that kind of stuff, because later on in life that is going to make you much more stronger. It is much more dangerous to have someone sheltered up and protected — as society really says to do with people with developmental disabilities — than it is to go through the pain and agony of a mainstream integration situation. And my father believed that. That's why they did it. Not only my father, my mother did, too.

He said, "You know, there's an agency. It's called the Regional Center. I think you should go down and apply and see if you could qualify for services."

I said, "Dad, I already have."

He said, "What?"

I said, "Yeah. A friend told me at work about the Regional Center, and I'm getting services now."

I said, "Dad, I want to tell you something that I never told you before ... that I think that I need to tell you."

He said, "Well, what's that?"

I said, "Dad, really, I'm grateful for what you've done — you and Mom — and I want to tell you that I really love you and care for you."

Our relationship started right then — from that moment on. I was about twenty-four years old. It should have started when I was younger and growing up, but it didn't happen that way. That's okay. What got me to that point of being able to have that relationship — like a father and son should have — is, number one, I got out of the house. I grew up. I needed to realize what I had as a father; number two, he needed to grow up in the way of letting me go. He did that, and Mom did that. He was finally glad to see me out of the house. He grew up a lot and started to appreciate a lot more things. He admired me a lot more. I wasn't the baby anymore that he thought that I wanted to be treated like. I was a grown man now.

We needed to go through what we went through, and that's how nature created a opportunity. So we started to be able to develop a son-and-mother-and-father relationship that no one can ever take away from us. It was the most perfect time.

I said, "Dad, I want to tell you something. I want to give my notice in my job."

He said, "Why do you want to do that?"

I liked my job, but I wanted to move back home, because all I really had was friends at work. I was lonely, frustrated. Things were not going well. And I picked up a bug, so I needed to go back home to be able to get well and to be able to catch up on some rest. That's what I ended up being able to do. Also, I think I just got burned out of the traffic and burned out of the city life. I had my thrill and joy of living in a great big city like San Francisco, and my dream was completed: I wanted to live in San Francisco, and I did — for two years. I experienced it; I had my experience living in San Francisco, and I wore out of it. I needed to go out and try a new thing and get my life going the way that I really wanted to. I always had to believe that I can do much better. It was just at a point where I wanted to come home and move on.

He said, "Well, you always are welcome to come home ... You're sure you want to do this?"

I said, "Yeah, Dad, I want to do this. I think I can get transferred up there to the Far Northern Regional Center."

He said, "How would you live?"

And I said, "Dad, I want to go on Social Security, welfare, SSI."

"Oh, no. You're not going to live on that."

I said, "Dad, lookit. I put into the system first, and I want to be able to take out of it now."

He said, "You got a valid point there. You could do that."

My father was saying, "You should go to Chico" — I think to keep the independence situation. And it was only forty-five minutes away from home, and they could come get me if I wanted to come home. It wasn't a really big, dramatic thing.

CHAPTER SEVEN

CHICO

I went ahead and put my notice in and I left. I moved to Chico, which is about thirty-five miles away from Red Bluff.

Mom helped me find an apartment. Was those apartments incredible! It was all apartments up and down the block — residential apartments and college students, but not the bad area where they always had parties. It was pretty calm. My grandma helped me move. My parents, I think, were in the middle of harvest. It was like in August.

So I came home and got a place in Chico.

When I go back to Chico on business, I always go by there, and I always cry, because that was the really first step of being able to have what I wanted. That was the beginning of the legacy of Michael Long — People First, and speaking, and all of that kind of stuff. It's a very special moment — a happy feeling, crying, of being proud of how far I've come. And I want to tell you ... I lived three other places in Chico, and I don't got any of the feelings that I do for that first place in any of those other three places that I lived in Chico. There's just this something about that area, that building. It means a lot to me.

They were brand new apartments, and they smelled great, and they were. The only problem was ... they had ants all over the place. There was ant hills on the bare ground when they started building, so the ants just got all over the place. They got into food, so you always had to call the spray man to come in and spray.

And I got on Social Security. That was okay with everybody. My father was really supportive. My mom was a little concerned about ... I'd be living on it for the rest of my life, and I would probably become lazy. I had to be able to prove that I won't become lazy from it. I wanted to work; I couldn't figure out what I wanted to do.

I went to the Social Security office in Red Bluff at the courthouse. They had a representative from out of the Redding office that came down and worked out of the courthouse at Red Bluff. I thought that it was good to apply in Red Bluff, 'cause someone was helping me to get through the paperwork. That was a person who is in charge of the day program for people with developmental disabilities. He and I had been longtime family friends. I went ahead and I applied, and I got approved because I was a person receiving services through the Regional Center. I told them I lived in Chico so they transferred my case down to the Chico office of Social Security, and I started receiving my check through that office.

I always had a purpose in life that when I went on Social Security I never believed I would live on it for the rest of my life. I always had a dream that one day I would get off of this. I kept that down deep inside of my heart. I was gonna just use this for a few years to be able to get set on what I can really develop in my life. One day I was going to get off it. I was very determined in that. I carried that with me.

* * *

Robert found out about a self-improvement course through a friend of his. He called me up and said, "Oh, Mike, you gotta come down to this training. It's incredible."

There are four different courses or trainings. He already went through the first one, and he was going through the second one as I was going through the first one.

In November of 1986 is when I took the training. I went down on the bus, and I stayed with Robert. He was still with that older couple. The course was held in a hotel — like a convention. The people that take the training usually are from the San Francisco Bay area. They don't stay at the hotel; they go home. In my course, there was 350 people; so there were a lot of people.

The thing that I liked about it ... it was a course where it was a variety of different backgrounds, and it was ages of twenty-one all the way up to sixty-five. We had a couple of people that were in their sixties. It was great.

How the course is ... you find out about all of the different backgrounds and how people put up with incredible lifestyles. The focus is how to be able to let go of your negative past or present and be able to focus on to getting the tools on being able to improve your life — the way of where you want to be able to be successful.

The cost made me think about it twice, but the trainers have doctor degrees in psychology. The way I looked at it is it's less expensive than going to see a psychologist.

'Cause I was living on Social Security at the time and SSI, Bob paid the $400 for the first one; then I paid him back. That was the first training. The second training was $800, and someone I met through the first training wanted to make sure that I continued on; so they fronted up the money, and I paid them back. The third training didn't really cost that much. Where it cost is being able to go down every Tuesday for three months; then there were three weekends, and that added up the cost situation. People in Chico were going down there already. I always got rides with them; so it was really cost-efficient for me. But it was a lot of money. If I ever had to do it again, what I would do is ... I would save the money up first. The reason for that is because I would feel more empowered and more responsible. I wouldn't have to borrow the money and make payments.

The question might come up: Did they pressure me into a situation where I had to borrow the money? And the answer to that is, no. No way. I made a clear decision that I wanted to take the training. I leaped and jumped into the situation, looking at avenues how I could take it now. I just saw a big difference in Bob's attitude and achievement. That's what really got me connected up with the training — seeing it making a difference in his life.

During the training there's certain exercises, and there's sharing time, then exercises, and more sharing time. Some of those exercises are self-improvement exercises. You get a partner and you ask questions. The psychologist helps people lay out the ground rules. Some of the exercises talk about your family members, and the psychologist walks around, and he listens and he gives advice to how to be able to dig out more stuff. It just gets all of the anger out of you — like you didn't understand why Mom grounded you at that time or that age. You get all of that frustration out.

What happens is it makes you connect to the people around you. It makes you go home and connect to your family, and say, "You know, I really understand, Mom, the time that you grounded me."

It makes you really want to be able to love and support and to be able to not have the mind-games-type-of-situation. I think that's why I connect up with my peers. Why I love my peers so much is because I understand that they've gone through a lot of pain and agony. It's a kind of crappy world out here. We don't have no control of what happens to us at times. We don't understand why we get grounded, but when we grow up, we start to begin to be able to understand all of that stuff.

Then, you have what you call "sharing opportunities." They last about twenty minutes long, and you form a line. By the end of Saturday, you're running up to the mike because everyone wants to go up there and share. You always are listening, and people gain from that listening, because you see how much in common that human beings really have together.

You say, "Wow, I'm not the only one that has a disability." It's just like the People First group.

By the end of Sunday, everyone has been up to the mike at least twice. When I got up and shared — I think it was on a Friday — I was up talking to the group, and I was saying, "I'm having a rough time. I don't like myself. I want to be ... this is what I want to be able to do: I want to be successful. I want to be able to be like everyone else. I want to be an incredible person."

I remember the trainer saying, "Do you believe that you could be an incredible person?"

I said, "You better believe I do."

He said, "So you do believe that you could be an incredible person?"

I said, "You better believe I do."

He said, "But do you believe it?"

I said, "You better believe I do."

People were starting to laugh.

He said, "But do you really believe it?"

I said, "You better believe I do."
Then he said, "You're lying."
I said, "Why?"
He said, "Who believes it?"
"Me!"
He said, "There you go."

In other words, what he was trying to do was to change "You" to "I." *I* better believe it. You see the reverse psychologist? I always looked at other people being able to think that I'm a incredible person, but down deep inside, I really didn't think that myself. But there's no one else that can be able to do it for you. You gotta do it yourself. So me ... if I believe it myself, that gives me the inner power to go out and achieve it. Then if I need assistance on the way to get there, then you ask for that. That's what I got out of that whole conversation, and that was about a five-minute conversation that took place.

So I had to be able to change the situation. I better start getting off my butt and quit running this sob story that I'm disabled. If I'm disabled, so what? So what if I'm disabled? I need to think, "So what?" Thinking that has done a really incredible thing. If I did not take this training at all, I would not be who I am today. I probably would have still felt that negative belief system — that I talked about — where I really haven't come out of my shell. I really started grasping and really believing that I was capable of doing things.

One of the things that I got out of the training — and this goes kind of into the meat of the training — the bottom line that I got out of the whole thing is: I am a capable and willing man. And every time that I look at a roadblock set in front of me at work or with anything in my life, I always look at the situation and always say: "I am a capable man of being able to deal with this. I am capable and willing to be able to handle this situation."

The training was about living your own life — knowing how you could be able to make a difference in your life and in other people's life, and being able to have your life in an incredible rich way where you're not just serving yourself, but you're serving others and making a difference in other people's lives. And that was just part of the growth — I have really come out of my shell.

* * *

I decided I needed to build a new structure, and that structure would look like a new belief system inside of me — how I feel about myself. I wanted to be able to start all over and do what Michael wanted to do in his life. That was another reason I left the Bay Area: I didn't think that I could be able to develop that down there. I needed a smaller community, like Chico was.

That's where I really started the foundation. Every, every morning — and I did this for about six months — every morning I'd look in the mirror, and when I look in the mirror I said, "I'm no different than anybody else. I accept who I am. I'm Michael. I'm okay."

I said to myself that I wanted to start to believe that I'm no different than anybody else; I'm the same as everybody. After repeating that over and over and over every morning for six months, that really built my belief system — getting rid of all of the negative crap that had happened to me between zero and twenty-four years old. The people at the motivation course, they didn't tell me to go home and do it. It came to myself to be able to do it. I did it myself.

Then I said that I want to change my image. I had a image for many, many, many, many years that people hated me because I was different. I was mentally retarded. I was disabled. And I was very angry. Very angry. So I had to get rid of that anger, and I had to change that image of people hating me when they really don't hate me. I needed to be able to accept them. I want a new attitude of being able to think, "People like me. People want to be around me."

So another six months, I started to say, "People want to be around me. People want to share my life. People want to know what's going on with me."

Then for the next six months after that, I said, "This is what I want to control my life ... " I just started building and building on that.

I had a big, strong belief system inside of me, and that belief system had to be able to change "I'm developmentally disabled" into "I'm okay." I needed a belief system where people believe in me, and they would support me in my effort and not say I can't do it. I had to get away from that.

Another thing that I need to do is quit giving and be able to start receiving from other people. I was the one that was always giving. I was the one saying, "No, I don't want nothing. I don't want to receive anything." So I had to be able to balance it out — to give, then to be able to receive. Giving, buying relationships — not only buying, but I always give myself up to be able to help other people out, and I never received. I was not a person who would receive anything back. I would not want anything back. I would not want to receive credit for what I did. I needed to change that, and that's what I did.

The new belief system started when I was twenty-four. I needed to start saving myself first, believing in myself and accepting who I am.

The emphasis was on making myself feel okay, but at the same time I was doing what I wanted to do for my life. It was like two to two put together as one — the things happened at the same time.

I wanted to build this new belief system and new self-image, and I wanted that to control my life. And at the same time I decided to set up a thing that I always wanted to do: I wanted to be able to be a 'quipment manager for a sports team. I heard on the news that Cal State Chico University was having a freshman football team developed. I went over at the university and talked to the coaches and asked if I could be the equipment manager.

The coach said, "Yes, we would love you to work here." They gave me a hundred dollars a month, but I was still living on Social Security.

Sports helped me to achieve my other goals in my life, because with sports you have not only the thrill and the agony of defeat, but you have those large crowds. It's great to be out in front of those large crowds. I'm a person that likes attention. I don't know if that's good or if that's bad, but that crowd noise really keeps me going to achieve what I want to achieve.

* * *

Driving was not the thing for me. I was so much in shape when I lived in Chico, because I always end up walking everywhere I went. Usually it takes fifteen minutes to walk from my house to downtown. I walked all around — I mean just everywhere. Everywhere. I hated waiting for the bus; I think I can get there quicker by walking.

I lived on my own for six years receiving a lot of life skills training two days a week, three hours a day. About six hours a week, I had a life skills instructor. During those six years, I had roommates. The last two years I lived with my uncle. My dad was the only child in his family and I only had one uncle that was on my mom's side. Uncle Glen lived with me in Chico.

The roommates connected up through the Regional Center. Case managers connected us up, thought we would be good and we would work out (these were other people with developmental disabilities).

Steve, one of my roommates, had autism. People never thought he'd be capable of living on his own. I was his role model — making that dream come true. He'd been in a care home for years and years; then he moved in with me. It was incredible. The problem Steve had was he loved numbers. He'd pick up the phone and dial numbers and ended up talking to people on the phone. Strangers. On the phone! Long distance!

He always talked about me, his roommate, to these strangers: "I got this crazy roommate. He thinks he's a really big shot, but I like him. He's a really nice guy. You know ... a really nice guy."

The people on the other line said, "Oooooh." And they'd say, "I gotta go. It was nice talking to you. I really appreciate being able to spend twenty minutes on the phone with you. Maybe I can call you back up, sometime."

When the bill came, he had to pay for it, and he was strictly on Social Security.

Steve was a great roomie. Then he decided to move into another apartment.

This Steve — this is the honest God's truth — I hadn't seen Steve for over two years, and I was visiting Robert one night. We just got home, and I went right into the restroom, and the telephone rings.

Bob said, "Hello?"

The guy said, "Is Michael Long there?"

Bob said, "Yeah. He's in the bathroom right now."

He said, "Can you tell him that I called? My name is Steve, and this is my number ... "

Bob said, "Okay, I'll do that."

So I got out of the bathroom, and I dialed the number. It was Steve. I never heard from him for two years, and lo and behold, he dialed Robert's number and said, "Is Michael Long there?" He had no idea I was there. He didn't know who Robert was or anything. And he called that number and asked if Michael Long was there. Pretty spooky ...

* * *

The next-door neighbors of that first apartment, they were three women that were college students at Chico State University. They were out of sight. Molly was one of the closest people to me in my whole life. She was like a mother to me. I wanted more than that, though! She always came knocking on my door to see if I was okay — if I needed anything.

I was so excited when she invited me over to dinner to meet her family. Her family just loved me and I loved them. I thought, *Oh, wow. Maybe this means something — that I can really start dating her.* 'Cause she was starting to come over more and more, and after meeting her family and all of that. It was just ... oh ... it was love at first sight!

I tried to date her, but it didn't work out. No one wants to hurt you. No one wants to hurt your feelings. Same old stuff, you know.

When I was taking the self-improvement training, I met this woman, and I really had a great big crush on her. Her name was Michelle, and we saw each other.

One night in my apartment in Chico I was in my bedroom and I had the light on and I had the stereo on and the station I turned on played her favorite song. After that a ghost of her shadow appeared, and it said, "Michael, you're okay. I honestly love you."

Then two seconds later, she disappeared. The amazing thing about the whole thing was she's not dead; she's still alive. When I saw her again and I told her about it, she was blown away.

Lyn was another person from the training. Lyn took the training with Bob, so she was ahead of me. We got to know each other, and we got to see each other a lot. Lyn was the particular American-blue-eyed-blonde-dream-woman. Lyn got so close to me. We always ended up seeing each other at different events in the third training, where we go out and have our friends enroll into the self-improvement course. We always got together and go out for coffee and just talk. And we'd talk about our lives. She was from St. Paul, Minnesota, and she was surprised to find out I had a bunch of cousins in St. Paul and Minneapolis and Duluth. I think that's what connected us up — when we started talking about where we were from.

The first time we went out for coffee it lasted for three hours, so it was really a connected situation. Then we started going out to breakfasts and stuff when I stayed over with Bob. I really started developing a lot of intimacy feelings and stuff. I was always excited and she was always excited to be able to see me and spend time with me. It was really going really well, and we were doing this for, I would say, for about six months. She was a dentist hygiene; so breath really mattered, and clean teeth really mattered. I cleaned my teeth, and I always had to have a mint to make sure my breath was really great and everything.

We started giving each other gifts because of birthdays and just appreciation of each other and our friendship. Because she lived in San Francisco and I lived in Chico, we started calling each other, also. We talked about once a week or twice a week; whenever she had an issue at work or when I had an issue, we went ahead and talked about it.

Then around the seventh month, I started saying, "I better really start going forward with this, and see where we would end up, and start laying my cards on the table."

One of the things I really got out of the training is honesty and communication, how you need to really communicate. So I asked her out.

It was a nice restaurant. I remember — I could see it right now — her reaction and what we were doing and everything. It's just really incredible. We met there. I went ahead and had a friend drop me off there, 'cause I wasn't driving. So we had dinner and everything. I was just on the high cloud, cloud nine, because this was a night that I thought was gonna be a night of really being able to get down to business, and being able to see where we were going with our relationship and friendship and everything.

We were having hors d'oeuvres, and she had a glass of strawberry daiquiri, and I had a virgin strawberry daiquiri. So we were eating hors d'oeuvres, and I said, "You know, Lyn, I wanted to be able to meet tonight, because we have gotten really close to each other, and I want to be able to develop something into a serious relationship-type-of-situation."

She said, "Michael, I'm flattered … but how can we do this when we live so far apart?"

I said, "I thought about that, and I just couldn't be able to come up with a good situation of me moving down here. The cost of living is really outrageous, and you know that I do have a disability and everything. I just don't have the college degree to really bring in a lot of money to be able to live down here."

She said, "Well, Michael. I can't move to Chico at all, because I'm really happy where I'm at and everything."

She said, "Michael, there's something that I want to be able to tell you ... that I been avoiding telling you for the last couple of months. That is ... I noticed how much we have really gotten close together and how we developed our relationship ...

"The thing is ... my vision for my family is that I don't want to have anybody that is developmentally disabled to be married to. The reason for that situation is because I don't know much about people with disabilities, and I don't think that it can really work. I know that we have really become really close to each other, but I'm scared, and I'm afraid, because I don't want to hurt you. I don't want to really hurt you and damage you, and I don't know if you could be able to handle the situation. I don't know if a person with a disability could handle a disagreement or a argument. And to me, it's really important that I have a person who has a college education."

It's the same kind of picture that Chasity gave me, the freshman I met in high school.

And — one of the things that was so incredible — she said, "Michael, I hope you're not angry at me for saying this."

I said, "You know, I want to be honest with you here. Before the training I would have been mad as heck, but now I understand this, and I understand your situation. One of the things that always happens to me is this situation: People without disabilities cannot understand people with disabilities. They don't want to go and date them because they don't think they can handle it.

"So I face it day in and day out. And it always got me angry inside of me, and now I don't feel that anger at all. I just feel relieved that we got this out in the open, and we know where to go from here.

"I won't think at nighttime about you — wondering when am I gonna get enough energy to be able to come and talk to you about this; or, I wonder if I should do it; or, I wonder if I should not do it. Should I just leave it alone and just be able to not deal with it in a honesty way?

"You know I'm glad that it's out in the open and I know where you stand. I love you for the way that you've approached this, and I want to tell you that you're the first one that I ever have said that I love you — for the way that you approached it, because in the past, I hated everybody else."

She said, "Well, I definitely want to still get together, and I definitely still want to be friends, but I don't want it to turn into a serious relationship where we could think about marriage, because I'm scared. I'm scared of being with a person with a disability."

I said, "Well, you know, that's the same with anybody. You'd be scared with anybody, but I understand."

We ate dinner, and we walked out, and she gave me a ride back over to Bob's house. Then she gave me the most incredible hug and kiss that I ever received in my life, up to then.

Three months went by, and we still kept in contact; then she moved away, and I haven't heard from her since.

* * *

The part of not being able to date a person without a disability was really frustrating. What is really wrong with me? Why does society put that on people — that you always have to go out for the top IQ in intelligence and looks? Why can't they look at personalities? Why can't they look at giving? Why can't they look at what the family is like? Family values? Everyone usually goes on physical attraction. There's a lot of angry feelings in not really being able to experience the relationship with a person who has a higher IQ or higher intelligence than I have.

Dating people with developmental disabilities ... what I found out about that is physical attraction is nothing. They go after all of the other things: personality, what the family's like. I think the reason why is because they've been begging for attention and love, and they want to experience that.

What is this thing of, *I always want to be a friend; I don't want to hurt you*? Like Chasity, the girl I met on the bus in high school after a track meet, and people like Molly at Chico State. In any relationship you're going to be hurt; that's just part of the risk.

People with developmental disabilities do not look at *You're going to be hurt*. They don't worry about what the person looks like. They don't go through all of that. What really counts is in the inside. Society is always worried about what you look like on the outside and not about what the person looks like in the inside. It's really sad that society makes people look at the situation like that, because they're the ones who are going to be losing, in the long run.

Also, one of the biggest hang-ups that our society has is — and this comes from inside, I think — is what you want to do with your life. For Chasity it was material things: "I gotta have a husband that has a four- to eight-year degree, where I feel secure that we will not always live on the street."

I think one of the biggest problems that we have is Hollywood. And frankly, to tell the truth, sports and athletics. They're really driven by the same kind of material things and being able to look at all that crap first. People look at what you got, and if you got something, material-wise, they think it's going to last forever. It's not to sound cruel or mean, but their day is coming.

* * *

I ended up dating a girl by the name of Donette. I met her through People First. She lived in Chico. She had cerebral palsy and she used a wheelchair. We developed this friendship, and we started seeing each other. She didn't drive, and I didn't drive, and we lived five miles apart from each other. I always walked over to her place, and I end up staying over there 'til ten o'clock at night, then I walked back.

I said, "Wow, I'm finally gonna be able to get involved with a relationship."

And Donette started noticing that I was getting serious, and she opened up to me and said, "Mike, I don't want a relationship. I'm afraid that I would hurt you. I'm afraid that we won't be able to be friends if anything happened to us. You could be my buddy. You could hang out with me. We can go out and do things together. But Michael, no, I don't want a relationship."

So what happened is: I ended up not seeing her for two years. Then we saw each other again at the health club where I started working. We made up for all of the angry situation — that I wanted a relationship so bad. I didn't want a friendship; I wanted to date her. I was so madly in love with her. So at the health club, we started hanging out again. I completely accepted there's no way that we're going to be able to date each other — that we're just buddies. It was hard to accept that.

She said, "The reason why we can't date each other is you're gone too much. You like to travel. I'm a home person. It just wouldn't work, Michael."

That was 'cause I started going all over making speeches. I said, "Yeah, I see your point. I understand."

She said, "Also, I want to be able to marry somebody who is not a person who receives services. I want an able-bodied person. I don't want a disabled person to get involved with."

I said, "I understand that."

Then came along Susie. She was a People First member. I think with Susie, too, my relationship was more of a companionship-hangout-buddy type of thing. We did a lot together, and we did not see any other people when we were seeing each other.

Then Susie decided to call everything off between us. I remember that day — it was the Fourth of July. We were just getting ready to go to the fireworks together, and we didn't go to the fireworks.

After that, I stayed single for about a year; then I met Misty. Misty was a person who lived about a half an hour west and south from Chico. My uncle lived with me then. He drove me all the time to go pick up Misty to bring her back to Chico, or I ended up staying over at her grandma's place where she lived.

Misty had a hearing-impaired disability. Also she had some cognitive disabilities — mentally retardation. Misty really made me feel like I really have blossomed in relationships — being able to know what it's like to be able to be in a relationship. Misty was a person who had a very open heart. Very caring. Very loving. Everyone thought we was such a perfect couple.

I could not believe that it was happening. We dated for two years, and we got engaged.

* * *

I was still keeping in touch with some of the people who I went through the training with — to kind of give each other support type of thing. What I did was I came out of one domain and went into another domain, where I'm not just serving myself but I'm making a difference in other people's lives.

Where I picked that word up, domain, wasn't through the training. Where I got that word, domain, is through a couple of people that took the training. They said that they can see in their lives that they have come out of a domain.

I said, "Well, what do you mean by 'domain'?"

They said, "What you mean by 'domain' is that you are in a specific area, and you build a bunch of stuff in your life, and it's good, and it's bad."

One of the things they said they got out of the training is to move in the area where it's enriching and where it's really in a new domain, of where you can make a difference in other people's lives besides yourself all the time. These two people, what their biggest hang-ups were — what society really put onto them: Me. Me. *Everything has to resolve around me* type of situation. That was their domain; so I understood what domain meant then.

I said, "Well, yeah, that makes sense."

I came to the course in the domain of where I was mentally retarded, and I felt mentally retarded. I wanted to be able to go in a new domain where I felt good. Not feeling good … you gotta watch out about feeling good about yourself. You gotta be able to improve on yourself. There's a difference. You really want to be able to do good for yourself, because if you just feel good about yourself … with feelings there's no solid foundation, and sometimes feelings go. What you want is more of a foundation. You want to always do good with yourself and build yourself up — each issue that you face in your life. Feeling cannot always make you move and grow, but it's the new domain that keeps you moving and growing. That's what I wanted, and that's what I wanted to be able to focus on. It has to do with a direction of outside yourself.

Being directed outside. I want people who believe in me and support me and my ideas to be in this domain. The people who don't believe in me, who say, "Oh, Michael, you can't do it because of this or this or this ... " — those people are in the old domain.

In the new domain, I want people on my side of the team who say, "Let's be able to do this. We gotta be able to face this and this and this and this to be able to get to that point, but we can do this."

I started looking at myself and how people believe in me and how I believe in myself. I want to be able to do what I want to do; I need to be around people who would support me with my ideas, not give me negative feedback that I can't do it. If I run into that situation, I'll develop the attitude: I'll show you that I can do it. That's how I got that — over the years. It took that long for it to come out that I would say, "I'll show you that I can do it."

CHAPTER EIGHT

PEOPLE FIRST

When I was leaving the Bay Area, I figured out that I did not want to do veterinarian work the rest of my life. I wanted to be able to challenge myself with something else where I could travel. That could be something with sports. It doesn't necessarily have to be something with sports, but basically, my main focus was I wanted to travel. So I wanted to get a job that I could be able to travel. If it's volunteer for a few years, that's okay. I'll live off of Social Security until I meet the right person at the right time, and I will get off. And I was determined.

Also, I started noticing that I need to get involved, somehow, with a support group with people with developmental disabilities. I had an independent-living skill trainer talk to me about this group in Chico called People First. He invited me to a meeting. I never heard about the group before.

Oh, I loved it. I loved it. I said, "Man, this is what I need," because I could relate to these people. "They gone through the same thing as I have." The reason why I felt a lot different is because I grew up and I realized that people with developmental disabilities are people too.

At the first meeting that I ever got invited to, they had elections that day. It just happened. I said, "So why not run for president and see what I can do?"

So I nominated myself, and everyone liked what I had to say. I said that I wanted to be a leader. "I want to include people. I want to be able to make sure that we have a good, strong group."

People loved hearing that, so they voted me in. There were twenty people. And so that's how I got in as president of People First.

* * *

The advisor of People First saw how I run the group. He was on the committee that nominates names for something called the Area Board — a board that watches over the Regional Center System. He sat down and talked to me and said, "Would you like to be on the Area Board?"

How the Regional Centers work is that they're a nonprofit corporation that is funded by the state that is able to provide services for people with developmental disabilities. One of the services are care homes. Believe it or not, they had twenty to forty living in a home. I call those mini-institutions. It's the same today — we haven't got rid of them yet ... all of them. Then you have your sheltered workshop where the Regional Center contracts out with the sheltered workshop to provide workday activity programs. They contract out speech therapy, occupation therapy ... Basically, they will provide any type of therapy, but the day programs and the sheltered-workshop type of thing is the biggest expense, overall, of the Regional Center system. Day program is where you have pretty significant people with severe developmental disabilities that comes through the day with different activities. Sheltered workshop, they work for piece rate through the day.

One of the things the People First movement and professionals in the field were starting to ask was, "Why are we paying all this money to be able to have people really babysit?" That's what they do is, basically, babysit everybody and not provide really good opportunities.

Then you got your other day programs where people should be able to have the opportunity to progress into the sheltered workshop environment and not just stay at the day-programs level. What the sheltered workshops provide is independent-living training. There is a lot of people with developmental disabilities who nobody, ten or twenty years ago, would ever think could be able to live out on their own. In recent years, there has really been a strong movement towards independent living.

So the People First advisor said, "I think you'd be awesome for this position on the Area Board where we need consumer input."

I got on the Board by a county appointment through the board of supervisors of the county. To have a consumer on the Area Board was brand new. The staff people at the Area Board were mad, because they wanted somebody else — another consumer — who they know all of their lives. They didn't even know who Michael Long was.

I started going to the board meeting. It took a while for the staff people to get familiar with me, but afterwards — after they got to know me — man, they were so happy, because that's where I really became a really strong advocate.

It took a while, but when my term was up, one of the staff members wanted me to be back on the Area Board of Directors. She wrote this nice, big letter of recommendation and I got reappointed.

All the stuff that I learned from Chris Bauer's civics class I really start putting into work right there. It was just amazing how it put things together and started developing all my skills that I learned from that class.

I got on the Area Board, and I started mentioning about People First. The staff of the Board thought People First wasn't going well and thought we need to be able to get the group going strong in each county. We need to re-energize it.

I said, "How do we do that?"

We decided to have our first conference for nine counties out of the fifty-two counties of California. That was the responsibility of the Area Board of nine counties. We'll start it up that way. We'll get people together at our first People First Conference in our region and talk about how to organize local chapters. I went to the meetings about planning this People First conference.

I decided everyone needs to know about this. It was my idea to be able to go around the nine counties. I start thinking, *How can I get some travel money and travel all over the nine counties and do speeches?*

Since I was an Area Board member, I found out I could use some of their money. That's when I really found out that I could do speeches. I had one of the staff people at the Area Board sit down with me and make a outline of what I need to talk about.

What I covered in those speeches is ... I talked about self-advocacy and People First: what we're doing, what is People First, and why are we doing it. Then I talked about the great big two-day conference and what it's about. I went to the schools and to day programs and shelter workshops to get people geared up to come to the conference.

The staff didn't think I was going around all the nine counties. At first they thought I was just staying in the Chico-Red Bluff area. Then I just started going hog wild. I started making all these appointments in the nine-county area. I called 'em up from the local office dealing only with retarded people, an organization, an association for retarded people. I hate that. I hate it. I hate that word "retarded."

We started planning it in July, and the conference was in March; so during the winter, I was going around doing speeches. The Area Board staff members thought I was crazy because of the weather and the snow and the way the bus transportation was all set up.

Then the Regional Center got in the middle of my plan. They got really concerned about someone taking advantage of me: *Do I know how to handle myself in the airport? Do I know how to check a airline ticket in? If there is a plane that is late, do I know how to handle that situation? Do I know how to check into a hotel? Do I know where to go and what to do?* ... All of this kind of stuff that everyone goes through. My brother and sisters had to go through that when they traveled — not only just a person with a developmental disability.

I had a IPP. That's an adult Individual Program Plan meeting, where you make goals for one year, and it always happens on your birthday. And they said I should be in a program type of situation instead of traveling all over the place. They thought I'm going to end up being hurt or I'm going to be ending up dead or whatever; so they were really not supportive of what I was doing.

So I said, "Lookit. Put some training things in. Let me learn how to be able to handle a crisis situation. What do you do if someone tries to mug you? Where can you call for help? How do you call for help?"

So they put some training in the IPP.

Then I decided it might not be a bad idea to maybe do the speaking and be on the Area Board and not work at Chico State anymore — speaking as a replacement for Chico State equipment manager — and have a part-time job in the afternoon.

So I said, "Lookit. I don't want no janitorial stuff. I don't want no lawn-maintenance stuff."

They thought that they could get me a job mowing lawns for the city and get piece rate. I said, "No, I got better skills than that."

They said, "So what are you going to do?"

I said, "I don't know. Let's figure something out. What can I do?"

So they referred me over to a job agency for supported employment. But then one day I walked in to join a health club, because they were having a special rate. There was this guy who worked with me at Chico State. He said, "Michael, you got a minute?"

And I said, "Yeah, what's up?"

He said, "I want to set up a appointment with you to see if we can hire you here. Would you like to work here?"

I said, "Yeah, that'd be awesome!"

He said, "Well, I can't promise you anything, but I want to hire you, and what I want to do is to see if you could be in charge of a program on hiring other people with disabilities. Then we'll have a crew of people with developmental disabilities working in a health club. Would you want to do that?"

I said, "Yeah! Yeah, let me know."

So I joined up, and he said, "Hey, instead of paying the money, why don't you put that on hold and let me talk to Scott about hiring you?"

Scott was the head boss who owned the sports club.

Scott said, "Okay, I won't charge him," 'cause people who worked there got a free membership.

I got a phone call, and he said, "Yeah, Scott said it was okay for you to come in to meet him."

"You mean, I get to meet a professional football player? You got to be kidding! This is awesome!"

Scott used to play professional football before he owned the health club.

"Yeah," he said, "he's really fired up about the program and he wants to do it."

I said, "Can you just give me Thursday and Friday off?" Because those were my days that I was with the Area Board — once every other month.

So he made it that I had Thursday, Friday, Saturday off. So I worked Sunday through Wednesday, and I did all my speaking on Thursdays and Fridays. Some of the time, I did 'em on Wednesday and Thursday, but I had to come into work at one o'clock. I couldn't have anything scheduled in the afternoon at all.

I found the job myself and then the job agency provided the support I needed at that job.

And so, man, I was set. I was rolling. I was happy. And this created this new type of belief system that I always wanted — that what Michael wanted to do, I'm going to show the world that I can do it.

* * *

Some of the areas where I did speeches did not have public transportation. And one of the speeches I did was for Lassen County, a town called Alturas, way up by the Oregon border. It's in the mountains.

I took the Greyhound bus from Chico to Red Bluff, spend the night at my mom's, next morning got on this mail route at five o'clock in the morning. I took a mail route from Red Bluff to a town called Susanville with the mailman. I would do speeches in the afternoon for a shelter workshop and for a school about the People First conference. After that, I would go eat dinner, and I would go see my friend and spend part of the night at my friend's house. I would get up at two in the morning to go catch a Greyhound bus to go to Alturas. I got there at 6 a.m., had friends meet me at the Alturas bus depot, take a nap, and that afternoon I spoke in Alturas. Then I stayed for a little while at my friend's house in Alturas to be able to catch the bus at twelve o'clock, midnight. And I would take it back to Susanville, and I would arrive in Susanville at three o'clock in the morning, and it was snowing! It was like five below zero. And I walked from the bus station down to my friend's house — about four blocks. Then at eleven o'clock that morning, I got a ride back from Susanville to Red Bluff from the mailman. Then, I took the bus from Red Bluff back to Chico.

I went and I spread the good news about self-advocacy and People First to school administrators, day programs, and shelter workshops. Since I was an Area Board member, I spent $1,000 out of their budget to cover the whole nine-county area. It took me about three months to circle the whole nine counties.

The first conference was a great success. Over 300 disabled people attended. So many people were involved in the conference, and many grew so much because of the involvement.

CHAPTER NINE

FORGING THE DREAM

After I went through all of the counties, I was asked to be a keynote speaker at the conference. When I got asked to be a keynote speaker, I didn't know what the heck I was doing.

An Area Board staff member asked, "What do you want to talk about?"

And we listed all the things out that I want to talk about — we did it in that way. They helped me put it together. This was the first time that I ever spoke to a large group like that, because usually day programs and shelter workshops and school administrators — they were small groups. The audience that showed up at the conference was 300 consumers with developmental disabilities and about, I would say, a hundred professionals.

This was in 1987 when the conference was, and it was in Redding. There was a speaker before me, and he was the Regional Center Director. Everyone was eating and talking while he was talking; you couldn't hear what he had to really say. Then I got up and spoke. When I got up there, it was the opposite. You could hear a pin drop in the whole place.

I talked about my life. It was about myself and about empowerment, about self-advocacy, what we need to do, how we need to grow, how we need to become strong advocates and start living independently, making choices for ourselves.

There was a story that I told about the squirrel and the electricity of the 240-volt wire, of frying the worker and myself and the squirrel. It happened in my sophomore year. We was getting ready for a youth group party at our house. Before they came out, our dog was just barking up a storm. I got tired of hearing the dog barking and so went out to see Carlos, one of our hired workmen.

I said, "Hey, why is that dog barking out there?"

He said, "Well, there's a squirrel in the irrigation pipe, and he wants to get the squirrel."

I said, "Well, why don't we get to the bottom of it? We'll lift the pipe up, and we'll have the squirrel come out, and we'll satisfy the dog of being able to have a squirrel for dinner and end it all, and forget this barking."

He said, "All right. Let's unload the stuff."

We unloaded the trailer where we load the pipe on when we take it out into orchard, and we found the pipe that the squirrel was in. We put the pipe underneath the wheel of the trailer, so we can lift it and the squirrel can come out the end that's up in the air and take off, and if the dog succeeded, he succeeded.

Well, what happened is when we lift that pipe up, we hit a 240-volt wire.

BZZZT.

It knocked both of us down, and it burned three holes in Carlos's shirt. I said, "Carlos, Carlos, are you okay?"

No sound or anything; I didn't want to touch him.

I said, "Carlos, Carlos, are you okay?"

He got up, and he said, "Yeah, I'm okay."

We got the pipe, and we found out that the electricity drilled a hole right through the pipe ... almost cut the pipe in half. When it hit that 240-volt wire, it shut the electricity off two miles north, south, east, and west. I mean, everything was shut off for about twenty seconds; then it came back on.

I said, "Let's go hook it up to the pump, over here, that we use for irrigation."

I thought, "Well, we could turn on that pump and have that water squirt straight out and drown the squirrel."

You wouldn't believe it — the squirrel was still alive! We were still alive! Everybody was still alive, but the pipe had a hole in it!

We turn on the pump. CHICKA. CHICKA. And that squirrel shot right out of there. That dog just went after that sucker, and he got him. So I fooled around with electricity; I learned a lesson.

I told that story — if I remember correctly — in the situation of that's how self-advocacy can be: If you get off your butt and get involved, self-advocacy can be that much strong, that strong, like lightning — a bolt of electricity. Yeah. That was the story that I used that night: Self-advocacy can be like the electricity of a 240-volt wire.

Everyone was looking at me, listening to everything that I have to say, and saying, "Yes, that is true. That's what I want. I want to be able to get to that point. How do I get to that point?"

After I was speaking, everyone just came up and swarmed me and just mugged me. Everyone wanted to be a part of my life. I was quite the famous person ... and I loved it. I mean, it was great. It was awesome.

That's where I said, "I finally found out what I need to do in my life — that is to speak. I need to speak about my life, to share my feelings about my life, to make a difference in other people's lives. I want to empower them to be able to get what I have as much as possible and be able to have a full society of true integration."

What really made me say I should do this is when I was starting to talk about my life at the conference. After all of that, after the first speech I did, I needed to go out and conquer the world. That was my mission. My mission also was to be able to get off Social Security and be able to get a regular job. The main agenda of the job would be changing the bureaucracy that people create in the system, holding people back from reaching their highest potential, and to be able to break the attitudes and to educate that, if you give someone choice and an opportunity, you're going to be able to see results.

One of the things I always, after I grew up, had a very strong belief in is being able to treat your peers as an equal — being able to include them and be a part of their lives. When you're up on stage, you have a tendency of being a little bit different than they are, because they're not always up on stage. So you always want to pull people — your peers — up on stage with you, making sure you're just as equal as everybody. I really believe that when you work together with your peers — with people with developmental disabilities — no one is any different than you are. You don't have no power over them, or they don't have any power over you. You should work together and be able to achieve the same type of thing in life.

I've always had that in my heart, and I think that's why people have a tendency of hanging on to me, because they see this great big teddy-bear-type-of-personality, and they want to be loved. I was a person that always gave that love, so I have a common language, I think, even with the person with the most severe, profound, developmental disability. Them and I have a common language together, and we can be able to communicate to each other. How I got that? I will never, ever know. It's a gift that I have, and I'm really grateful to be able to have that gift. I don't want it ever to go away.

I think the reason why it took a long time to see other people same as you are — with a disability — is because I never really accepted myself for who I was. And I think you've really got to — before you can be a person in the limelight in the movement. You got to be able to, first of all, believe in yourself and be able to accept yourself, because if you can't accept yourself, you won't be able to accept other people around you. It's going to be more of a competition-type-of-situation, instead of working together in harmony. It took me twenty-four years to be able to accept who I was.

* * *

When I got hired at Chico Sports Club, I wanted to start speaking at other conferences around the state — different People First conferences and professional conferences. So the Area Board let me start speaking and the Area Board would pay for my way. I started by volunteering my time speaking at Chico State University. I did a bunch of speeches at Chico State and different elementary schools and junior high schools. I totally enjoyed the public speaking. I had a lot of fun. I really only had about one or two different speeches when I was volunteering. I just sat down and made an outline of things. I just looked off of that outline and started talking to the groups. I got the storytelling from my grandfather — being able to tell the different events that have happened in my life comes from the side of my grandfather. He always had a fish story to tell. And so, I loved it. I loved it.

Usually when I do speeches, it's a lot like a roller coaster. A half an hour before I go speak, I'm at the bottom. I'm at that low, low stage, where no one can draw on you. No one can really talk to me at all. I'm getting prepared. I can't interreact. You couldn't be able to withdraw any information from me. You can't talk to me, because I'm so emotional down at a level where people could not even understand. I'm just at peace with myself, and I think the reason why that is, is because of sharing my life experiences in those speeches.

It's a climbing up. When I start off with my speeches, you're going up this hill; then when you're done with questions and ready to get in the car — ready to go home — suddenly it's a drop-off straight down like a roller coaster ride. You always end up climbing high, and then you're always coming back down to where you were when you begin the speech. It's a 'motional roller coaster ride.

* * *

I found my little niche, and that was public speaking. When you do a lot of talking, you're gonna build your vocabulary up. I don't believe in IQ testing, but when I became a person to receive services through the State of California, my verbal skills on the test was a seventy. And when I moved to Sacramento in 1991, they wanted to re-test me again. The overall score was sixty-eight in 1985. That made me qualify for services — you had to have a score of seventy or lower. When they test me in Sacramento, my verbal skills jumped from seventy all the way up to ninety-nine. So you can be able to see the difference, because of the skills I earned from public speaking and from self-advocacy.

* * *

I went to a lot of different conferences around the state: People First conferences and supported living conferences, different type of professional conferences. People started really connecting with what I had to say. That gave me a lot of training in preparing for speeches and being able to be more human, down to earth, being able to draw people in to what I had to say — to really change the system and to really make a impact. Case managers always look at — I get this from parents also — "Oh, Michael ... he's capable of doing anything. My child is not capable of doing that," or, "My person that I serve is not capable of reach that potential."

So I think being able to get rid of all the pre-judgments that social workers come up with (through their textbooks that they study with), and being able to consider taking a little risk, gives people opportunities of being able to reach their farthest potential.

In 1991, I went and spoke at a People First conference in Santa Barbara; Denny Amundson was a speaker there also. This was the first time Denny and I ever met each other. As the keynote speaker, I spoke first; then Denny spoke right after me. There was an hour-and-a-half session, and we split the time. Denny was just watching me, as I was doing my thing and telling my story.

I remember, his first remark was, "I'll never do this again — having a consumer speak before I do."

Afterwards, he came up to me and said, "Michael, I want to be able to talk to you."

I said, "Yeah, let's go outside and talk."

He said, "Let's have a cup of coffee at lunch and talk then."

I said, "Okay." So we did that.

He said, "Michael, we're creating this new position at the Department of Developmental Services, and nowhere in the United States — or maybe even in the world — it's never been formed. It is where the governor would be hiring a person with developmental disabilities, and they would be able to travel all over the state and advocate for people with developmental disabilities."

Oh," I said, "that's what I've always dreamed about. Oh, it'd be great!"

He said, "Well, Michael, I want you to be able to apply for the position."

I said, "You got to be kidding."

He said, "No, I want you to seriously think about it. You would have to move to Sacramento, and I think you could do that. But I want you to think about it. Go home, send your resume in, and we'll get working on it."

Denny and Governor Pete Wilson got together, after Denny got approved by the Senate's Rules Committee and after the governor signed off.

Denny said, "I want to be able to create a position where people that receive services through our system would be able to give a power voice from their perspective."

Governor Wilson wholeheartedly approved it.

And so what Denny did was, he created not a job description, but a foundation of the position. And Governor Wilson had to be able to approve it, and after he approved it, Denny would be able to start collecting names and to start looking around for that person. So they started going through the interview process. You had to go through an interview at the Department; then you had to go through a interview at Human Health and Welfare Department. After that, you had a Governor's Appointment Secretary interview through the governor's office. Then after that, the governor signs off on it — if he okays it. That was the process of being able to have the first Consumer Coordinator position.

* * *

My father died when I was in Chico. It was August 15th, 1991, and it was a second Thursday of the month. Prune harvest was just ready to begin the next day. I was dating Misty at the time, and Misty and I decided to go up to Red Bluff to have dinner on a Tuesday night with my parents. He and I got in a big discussion about retirement. I was telling him that he needed to slow down and start thinking about retirement, because he's not going to be here much longer if he doesn't slow down.

He said, "You never tell me what to do! I will do what I please, and I will retire when I want to retire. And it's none of your business!"

I mean, he went on and on and on and on. I thought he was just going to lay right into me — right there. It was great. It wasn't great then, but I think it's great now. That was the last time I saw him.

My father was a workaholic, and he was getting up in age — he was fifty-seven. He needed to start thinking about retirement and quit working so hard as he was. Slow down; maybe cut out all the commercial work and just keep the land that he has, take care of his places, and just slow down.

He wasn't having health problems. I just wanted him to slow down. But Dad loved to see the trees grow. Dad loved to harvest the trees. Dad loved to drive the tractors around, haul them here, haul them there. He loved to turn on the irrigation pumps. He loved to spray. He loved to do all the things that farmers do.

He always got mad when anyone mentioned the word "retirement." He always went up and told his parents about it. That was always the outlet. His parents were still alive. They lived two miles away; he always stopped by there and blew the whole thing off on Grandma and Grandpa.

I think this is why I really handle my father's death: That Tuesday night, Misty and I had dinner with my family. After we ate dinner and we said goodbye to Grandma and Grandpa, I said, "Dad, I'll see you later. I love you very much, and I'll see you soon."

Those were my last, departing words to him. I said it, and we drove off and went back to Chico. My uncle drove us. We drove Misty back home.

Dad took the next day off and spent the day with his grandkids, because it was one of the grandkids' birthday — one of Nancy's kids. Mom and him went down to Stockton, and that day I went for my second interview down at the Department in Sacramento. My uncle gave me a ride down there. So what happened is, I got home, and I left a message on Mom and Dad's machine, saying, "The interview went really well. It really looks like it's going to happen. I got one more interview to go through, and it looks really good."

The next morning at eight o'clock, and I can't remember where I was heading to, but I was heading out to somewhere. My brother caught me just in time. I remember exactly what happened. I lived in my fourth place in Chico — upstairs on the second floor. This apartment complex in the center had a swimming pool and a great big yard. It was beautiful landscaping and flowers and everything. Over by the pool there were two or three friends that I knew. I came down the stairs, talked to them; then I started walking out towards the city bus.

My brother approached me and said, "Mike, I got some sad news." He never stopped off to see me; he made a special trip.

He said, again, "I got some sad news … Dad's been killed."

I said, "No! No!" I just went really berserk.

I said, "How?"

He said, "He got hit by a train. He was killed instantly."

And I said, "No! That can't be."

The three friends came running over to see if I was okay.

I said, "I gotta go. My father just died."

I stopped what I was doing and went up and got some clothes, and I went home with my brother.

Greg didn't drive. A friend drove Greg down to pick me up and take us back.

What happened is … Dad went to one of the orchards about forty minutes away from the house. He was going to turn on an irrigation pump. He was dressed up for a Board of Directors meeting for the Northern California Production Credit Association that was in Chico. He decided to take a shortcut to Chico because he was running late. On that shortcut there was a crossing, and that crossing didn't have no guardrails to come down, because it was out in the country, and there's not enough traffic on the road to have guardrails. So it had a stop sign. We don't know what exactly happened. There were some limbs that were sticking out that could have blocked his view. The train hit him at forty-five-miles-an-hour impact. There was a little creek and a bridge for the railroad track. He took out that whole bridge. I'm sure the pickup rolled a couple of times, and he was thrown out of it. It was nothing left. It was a one-ton Dodge Ram pickup that had forty gallons of diesel, and some of that leaked out alongside the tracks. Nobody was hurt on the train.

Arriving at home, there were fifty people met us. And all of 'em were just standing around, standing outside the door in shock — just totally in shock. I could not believe it … just could not believe it at all.

I remember the first thing that happened: Greg and I walked

up, and Kathy and Nancy were right there. All four of us were holding on to each other with probably a lot of fear, a lot of anger, and a lot of frustration.

After, we sat down and talked about where we wanted to have the funeral, what we wanted to do, what should we do, and what was his favorite verses out of the Bible, and planning for the memorial service, and calling all the relatives from Nebraska and Seattle, Washington. I couldn't believe all of the phone calls from high school football coaches, basketball coaches, Regional Center people, Area Board members, consumers ... and people in the People First group.

We have thirteen Regional Area Boards in California; Chico is in Regional Area Two and People First is a regional group for that Area. Everyone in the People First group knew Dad, because my mother always had the planning retreats at our house. There were thirty people each year for three weekends to plan the conference, so a lot of consumers knew him and loved him.

Not only Dad was on the school board, but he was a volunteer fireman for thirty years. Twenty years he was the chief of the volunteer fire department, so he saved many, many lives over those thirty years. I mean really a community person. I remember all the people that came over during the next four days.

I was really determined to go by the accident and no one would take me there. So my uncle finally showed up. I remember that I said, "Hey, Glen. We gotta go find that pickup. You gotta take me to that accident — where it is."

He said, "Mike, we can't find that pickup."

I said, "Glen, we're going to find that pickup."

I had to go see it. So the next morning, Friday, we drove around, and we saw the place where the accident was.

A guy who gave me a ride sometimes, up to the college, met us. He just showed up; we didn't have any plans to meet out there or anything. He was trying to figure out how it happened. He's a specialist in accidents; he goes out and investigates accidents. He couldn't figure it out.

I said, "Hey, Dave. You gotta do me a favor. You gotta tell me where that truck is."

He said, "Mike, you don't want to go see that truck."

I said, "Dave, do me a big favor. Tell me where that truck is."

He said, "Well, it's down here on the corner of Los Molinos at a junkyard shop."

I said, "Thanks, Dave. You probably saved my life from going crazy ... if I didn't know where the truck was."

So later on, my uncle and I went over to find the truck, and we found the place. The guy who owned the junkyard shop wouldn't let us in. He said, because he's been in this business for forty years and with this kind of accident, he said, people have been screwed up all their lives after they see this truck.

I said, "Sir, I gotta see the truck."

He said, "I'm sorry. I won't let you in, because it's gonna foul your life up."

I said, "Sir, I'm gonna jump that fence — climb over it — and if you have to call the cops, go ahead. I'm gonna go over that fence and see that pickup, because you don't know what my life is like after, if I see it or if I don't see it."

I finally scared him a little bit, and he let us go see the pickup. It was incredible. That whole thing — from the engine to the steering wheel – was all the way back to the back bumper. Everything just crushed but the back bumper. Just demolished. Just demolished. Nothing left.

I needed to see it to get completed. That was the way to get completed. Something that's really weird about this ... my sister Kathy, my brother Greg, my foster sister Becky, and Nancy — they all have had nightmares about a pickup being hit by a train. It went on for months. And I don't have one dream yet.

I think the reason why I accepted the death of my father so well is because of the training — of being able to see the situation through the training: that Michael is capable of handling things in today's world.

Also, I think what made a big difference was the one thing that I wanted most of all in my whole life is peace. I mean, just being able to know that there is gonna be rough times, but the most important thing I wanted in my whole life is peace — just a mellow peace over me. One of the things, I think, why I handle my father's death so well is because I came to a understanding that my father was at peace, and that I'm at peace, too, with it.

Also the reason why I was so settled and peaceful is because I got to say goodbye to him. No one else got to say goodbye. Mom ... she just couldn't believe it. She kept begging for him to walk through the kitchen door and said she just wanted five minutes with him. That first night we all stretched across the bed — all of us lost without him. Mom had a hard time returning to the bed. She slept on the sofa in the living room for months. She was so saddened and upset that it happened. But she's a really strong person in faith, and she knew harvest was coming and life had to go on.

That harvest was the most difficult harvest of all. It was going to start on that Friday, but it didn't start 'til Tuesday. Everyone started to come in on Saturday and Sunday, and the memorial service was on Monday.

It was something like at 2 p.m. I remember getting in the car with the family members and driving into Red Bluff. Luther Street is about, I would say, three-fourths of a mile to a mile long, and at the end of this street, on the right-hand side, was the church that my family went to as we grew up. We made a turn onto Luther and all you saw — three-fourths of a mile — was cars all lined up. On the left-hand side there was another church, and that whole parking lot was full of cars. Misty and her whole family came. We saw people walking down towards the church.

That really made me say, "This is real, folks. This is real."

It kind of hit me and woke me up.

There was over 900 people that showed up for the funeral. Red Bluff is 11,000 people, so 900 is pretty incredible. There were people even standing outside: The building couldn't hold any more people, and they had to put speakers outside. The town was in shock for about two years — people still saying, "I can't believe Dudley's gone."

One of the most scary moments of the situation happened when we were trying to get ahold of one of Dad's best friends, another farmer he did a lot of business with. We were trying to get ahold of him to be a pallbearer. When he heard about the accident, he left town; never showed up until the funeral. He couldn't take it. He just could not take it; he was in shock. He was in disbelief. This really woke up a community — 'specially the farming community — in the situation of ... they need to start thinking about retirement and not working as long hours. Life can be taken away ... just like that.

There was this really neat family and they had a daughter had Down syndrome. When she was a little girl, their house caught on fire. Dad went in and helped save their belongings and gave her and her mom a big hug. That kind of tells you what kind of guy he was. No matter what, if it was a Down syndrome person or if it was a person without any disability or anything, you know he'd risk his life to make sure that they were okay.

So Dad was her hero; she always looked up to Dad. We tried to reach her family and tell them about Dad's death, but the grandmother, and the mother, and the person that had Down syndrome — she's an adult now — they were in Monterey having a little family vacation. The father stayed home. When John, the father, heard about it through the newspaper, and he called and told his wife about it, and they decided to come home early.

They said, "Well, we're not going to tell her about the death. We'll wait until we get home, or we'll tell her on the way."

They started on the way home and they said, "You know why we're going home early is because … "

She said, "I know why we're going home."

She stopped her mom from talking.

She said, "Dudley Long died."

We will always wonder how she knew that he died. Her mom couldn't figure it out, because she was never around with the phone call.

During the memorial service, we had open mic for all the people out in the audience to share what they knew about Dad — what they liked about Dad.

I didn't talk at the funeral, but it made me remember Dad having a discussion with somebody in Chico. The guy he was talking to owned a machine shop that helps build hullers. And they were talking about owning businesses and stuff.

The thing that I remember most of all was how my father said to him, "You know there's just no way, Bill, that I would be able to work for somebody like you or somebody else."

Dad said, "I always wanted to be my own boss. I never could work under anybody. I gotta be my own boss. I gotta be independent. I gotta do that."

That's why he picked farming.

The church people, and a lot of other people who knew Dad, had a great big potluck after the funeral. And it was in a church basement, and a lot of the people stuck around. We never got out of there 'til about eight o'clock, eight-thirty. Dad would really want that. Dad would really get a kick out of that whole situation and all the stories that was told. Dad would just be laughing — I mean, really laughing at the whole situation. I mean it was really a sad situation, but people made it funny — not funny about the death — but funny about telling the stories that Dad pulled on everybody.

One of the biggest stories that I remember is ... when he was a kid he had a Sunday school teacher who hated snakes. She hated snakes, and he always had this toy rattler. In Sunday school he always rattled it while she was teaching, and it always made her jump. So one time what he did to her was he put rocks in her hubcaps.

She said to her husband, "What's that noise in the car?"

"Well, I don't know what it is! Let's pull off and see what it is."

So what happened is she went ahead and pulled up the hubcaps and there were a bunch of rocks in the hubcaps. She knew right away who did it. She decided to get a tray and serve rocks for dessert for Sunday school class. She just greased 'em up a little bit like black candy, and she made sure Dad got the first pick.

So Dad took a bite and said, "What are these?"

"Those are the rocks you put in my hubcaps!"

* * *

After Misty and I got engaged, there was a big thing that happened between the family and I. I saw her on the weekends, because by then I applied for my license when I moved down to Sacramento. I heard about hand controls — I drive with hand controls and everything. I got the hand controls in April of 1992. Drew Rehab Department and the Regional Center both, that's how I found out about that. Drew Rehab Department is a driving school for people with hand controls. I went to a special school to test for it; then I went to the official officer of the DMV District and talked to a judge for the Department of Motor Vehicles. She signed off that I'm legally able to drive in the State of California under these conditions ... on my driver's license.

Misty and I were in the middle of the discussion of if we want to have kids. Misty was capable of having kids, and if we were going to get married, what should we do?

Her family did not want us to have kids. That got in between us, and it ended the relationship. Misty was pulled like a rope in between me and her family. She could not handle it. She didn't know where to go.

And the bottom line was: She said, "Mike, I'm sorry. I'm not going to give up my family and have them turn totally against me."

That ended up calling off the marriage.

* * *

When I moved to Sacramento from Chico, it was a risk-taking situation of where I did not have the job yet. I wanted to move to make a statement that I was serious about this and move the process along faster. But I want to tell you, there for four months, all I did just about every day was go and see a movie ... for four months.

Denny said, "You're nuts! I know it's going to happen, but you're nuts moving down here before you got it."

He said, "I'm not discouraging you that it's not going to happen at all, but you should have waited until — "

I said, "I'm on a vacation."

I remember that Denny was telling me that I should enjoy my vacation, because I wouldn't have another one until a year after I started. All I did is went to see movies — matinee movies at the one-dollar movie theaters.

I lived in a house that rent was a hundred dollars. That house was owned by some friends of mine in high school that were in Nancy's class. I really loved being on vacation, but I was scared. I was really scared, because I didn't know what I was going to end up doing — what was going to happen to the job. At this time, I was still living on Social Security and SSI.

Then, finally, in April we got the news that it happened: Michael Long was the first governor appointee in the United States, as a person that received services through the field of developmental disability. Starting salary was $24,000 a year.

I was back at my parents' house visiting my girlfriend at the time when I got the phone call. I was really excited. I was just so shocked, I couldn't believe it. I couldn't believe my dream had started coming true, that I'll have a opportunity to be able to prove to myself. That I can be a taxpayer citizen like everybody else.

I remember Denny was saying, "When do you want to start? Do you want to start Monday morning, or do you want to start Friday?" Which was tomorrow — he called on Thursday.

I said, "I'll be there eight o'clock in the morning. I'll see you then."

I was so excited and so thrilled. I couldn't believe it. I thought, "Man, I just won the Super Bowl."

After I drove back, I was really excited about being able to get started. I walked in that morning, and there was a bunch of candy and cards and everything — "Welcome to the Big Bureaucracy World" or something like that. I was so nervous; I didn't know what to do. I remember my first secretary, Sharon, welcoming me to my new job.

Then Denny came in and gave me a great big hug, and he said, "Well, how'd you like your candy?"

I said, "Just what I needed."

The next person came in, and it was another colleague on the executive staff that I'm going to be working with a lot. She gave me a great big hug and said, "You made it! You made it!"

I said, "Well, what do you guys want me to do? I don't have nothing to do."

Denny said to the woman, "Why don't you take him to your staff meeting today and introduce him to everybody? That'll take two hours up out of the eight."

I said, "What do I do for the other six?"

And he said, "Don't worry about it; we'll figure something out."

So I was sitting down and observing everybody and everything, and I said to myself, "Yeah, this is bureaucracy — sitting down and talking about all the different things and everything. This is red tape! This is a lot different than what I'm used to at the local level."

I said, "Man, you've been working on that *that* long?"

It was amazing. That person said they had a project and how long it has really taken them and how hard they worked. It was really a great education, or an eye opener, how long it really takes. I mean that because of how long it took for my appointment to happen.

Then I took a tour around. Denny really didn't know what I could do, 'cause this was a new job: No one had a job like this at all — anywhere in America, and we even think in the world. It was a brand-new thing.

So I started. One of the most exciting things that happens is ... every Monday morning there's what you call "executive staff." It's where all of the top eight people get together and share about what is happening at the management level in their offices ... being able to share information back and forth and being able to make sure people know what's going on at the management level.

And I was part of the executive staff.

There was a person who was responsible for the Regional Centers, a person who was responsible for the attorney's office, another person is head of the budget department, a person who was responsible for legislation, a person that was responsible for public media, a person that was responsible for the developmental centers, and another deputy that works with sixteen unions. Then there's me.

My job title was "Consumer Coordinator." It was hard to get used to that, because now I'm in a whole, completely different world. I'm trying to still be a person with a developmental disability; then here I got this plush job with the title, and of all my peers never had the opportunity to have a title like that. It was very hard to be able to accept to have a title under my name. I didn't want to be the first one, but I was the first one.

It's still hard to accept. It's a everyday type of thing that you gotta be able to get over that, that "you got a title" situation, and to remember: Don't let that control you, and don't let that build your ego up, and remember that you are still the Michael Long that you were when you were living in Chico and San Francisco and Red Bluff.

The job description they had for the person who got the job is: a consumer who would provide advice to the Director on all matters related to consumers. (I didn't have any trouble with that.) Assist in creating and coordinating meetings and activities for Consumer Advisory Committees. (I didn't have any problem with that either.) To be able to advocate for and assist the creation of a statewide advocacy group such as California People First and local consumer groups. (And I didn't have any problem with that.) Giving speeches at conferences, seminars and training sessions. Identify training needs. Assist in providing training and developing training material. (I didn't have any trouble with that either. One of the things I did was I created a manual for public speaking training.)

With consumers throughout the state, I had to find out what they need and what they want and provide input from consumers' perspective. The Department didn't know how I was going to be able to do those type of things. So it was very vague, that part. I didn't have no lead where to go, so I put my thinking cap on. I decided to create my own job description. So I just went out and started doing everything that I think I should do — being able to create Consumer Advisory Committees statewide: one for each of the twenty-one Regional Centers and also going out and visit their meetings and bring information back to the Department — to really get some great services and get some great-quality results out of people.

I said, "Well, what I'll do is go out and do a lot of public speaking on awareness about people with developmental disabilities." I would go out and not only do elementary and junior high or high school awareness, I would also go to Cal State University and do training for students who are studying at being special education teachers, and talk about mainstreaming and integration and how to be able to work that out in the situation.

I decided to go around to each Regional Center and help them develop a Consumer Advisory Committee at the local level. How I did that is I got some thoughts together on what kind of issues they could be working on with the Director or with the staff person at the Regional Center level. It would be local consumers in those Regional Centers that would be meeting with the staff member or with the Director of that Regional Center that they get services at. Then I created a lot of People First groups out in the community. How I did that is I went and talked to administrative staff in the developmental centers — inside the institutions — about the importance of self-advocacy and empowerment. I planned to come back and do an empowerment training for all consumers.

Then I would go talk to the staff first, and then I would come back and talk to consumers. Then a lot of consumers got involved with it, and now all of the developmental centers have People First groups. Now consumers are participating on local boards and even state boards — after getting involved with People First. In fact, Governor Wilson not only appointed a person with a developmental disability to be part of his staff, but he also appointed — for the first time ever in California history — a person that lived in the institution to be on the local Area Board in that institution area. So Governor Wilson really made a big effort to include the most severe people with developmental disabilities.

Denny loved my plan that I adapted to the job description, and he said, "Go for it — all the way."

There was a few people that was resistant, but I would say, overall, they were excited about the situation. Another thing that's really sad ... I believe we had somewhere around 300 employees at the headquarters of the Department of Developmental Services. What is really sad is that there were people in the headquarters of 300 people still didn't even know my office exists. But there was an all-day in-service for the whole Department, and I was a speaker at that. I had went to Austria and Germany and Italy to talk about starting up People First groups, and I spoke about my trip. And that opened the doors of being able to have the Department being aware of having a person who's receiving services from the Regional Center that is working at the Department.

CHAPTER TEN

THE AMERICAN DREAM LAUNCHED

After the relationship situation with Misty ended, I decided not to date for a while. Six months later, I called up a friend of mine that I knew for about six years. Her name was Hallie.

I met Hallie in October of 1986. She came up in '86 to look at the junior college up in Quincy, and that was up near Lake Tahoe — up in the mountains. She had a friend that was on the planning committee who wanted her to go to the college. So what happened is Hallie came down to look at the campus and then got asked to come down to the planning committee of the first People First conference. Hallie and I met at the retreat at my family's house; this was the second planning retreat out of three of 'em for the conference. Hallie had a crush on me right away. I had to be polite, so I went ahead and gave her my number. She kept in contact with me and called me about once a month all the time throughout the years — just wondering how I was doing. It was her effort. She hung in there for six years before I even batted a eye on her.

Then I said, "Man, look at what I got! Look at what I been missing!"

So I started driving out to Quincy; it was three hours away from Sacramento. Hallie and I started seeing each other, but I didn't know what I wanted. Then the amazing thing was ... she called me up and she said, "Michael, I'm planning your Thanksgiving for you."

I said, "Wait a minute. What are you talking about?"

She said, "I want you to come down and meet my family."

I said, "Now, wait a minute, Hallie. You can't do this. I got plans to be able to go and be with my family."

She said, "But Michael, I want you to be able to come and meet my family, and I want them to meet you. I want you guys to be able to get to know each other."

I said, "Well, I tell you what. I'll think about it — under one condition. Next week UCLA and USC are playing a football game." (It's the big rivalry of college football.)

I said, "You get tickets to that game, and I'll come."

She said, "Okay. That's a deal."

I thought, *There's no way she's gonna be able to get tickets the week before that game ... "*

Lo and behold, she got tickets. So I had to be able to follow up on my agreement to come down.

I fell in love with the family. The family was just really great. I woke up a little bit more when I went and visit the family. I loved Hallie's sister and brother-in-law. That was really important to me. And Hallie's mom — I really love her.

So at Christmastime I was down there in L.A. at her parents' house again, but we didn't have any time to really talk about engagement or anything. I forgot all about to make time to really sit down with Hallie's parents and say, "I want to marry your daughter," and, "I love your family."

It's really important to get along with in-laws; to me it's really important. So Super Bowl weekend, we went out to dinner in Sacramento. She was on her way home from L.A., and I picked her up at the airport, and I was going to take her up to Quincy.

I said, "We'd better get this out of the way right now: I probably can't do it on Valentine's Day because of snow and all of that."

I had went out and bought a engagement ring. I had the ring on me and everything. She didn't have no clue that I was gonna ask her. No clue at all.

But I forgot about asking her parents. So I said, "Hallie, I gotta go use the bathroom." We were in a restaurant of a hotel.

She didn't really believe that, because I was smiling at the time. She was like, "Right!" Hallie said, "Okay." But she really didn't believe me that I was going to the bathroom. She thought something was up.

I thought, "I'll go to the phone and call her family up and discuss this with them and say, 'You know, I had the intent to talk to you at Christmas, but I didn't get to; we ran out of time. I need to be able to get this out of the way, because Hallie is here right now and I want to be able to deal with it.'"

I went to the phone, and I called her mom up. I said, "Roselynn, this is Michael. I wanted to know if I could be your son-in-law. I want to marry your daughter."

She said, "What?! No. No. No. You got to be kidding!"

I said, "Yeah! I am not kidding. I want to be your son-in-law. I didn't make time to talk to you at Christmas; I meant to do it. I wanted to ask you in person, but I didn't make time to sit down and really talk."

She said, "You got to be kidding. Is this a crank?"

I said, "No, it's not a crank."

Then, here came Hallie, watching me, spying on me.

I said, "Tell your mother that it's not a crank!"

She said, "Guess what, Mom? I'm getting married!"

Hallie had to hold the phone clear out, and you could hear her mother screaming her head off — you know — just so shocked and surprised and everything.

So we called Hallie's sister; same thing happened. The whole family was like that. She freaked out; she just couldn't believe it. She was really excited, and she said, "Michael, I want to tell you something: You don't know how much this means to me. You're so great to my sister. All our lives, we didn't think that she would get married. To be able to see this as a reality is an incredible situation."

So there were a lot of tears on the phone. I think there were more tears by Hallie's sister than there was by Hallie's mom.

One of the things that really was amazing ... both of our families never dreamed about us getting married. No one in the world would be able to have us as wife and husband. No one would want that situation, because how we were segregated in the world situation. We always had a belief that they didn't think that we were capable of getting married, that it would never happen to neither of us. That's why it was such a shock to her mom.

Then we went to another hotel; it was a nicer place than the one we were at. We should have gone there for dinner, but it didn't work out like that. At this second hotel, they had a three-sixty circle with great big windows looking out on a manmade type of pond. In the center of that pond there was a fountain that shot straight up, and underneath that fountain there were different lights to make the fountain look different colors. It was a pretty romantic place to be able to ask a person.

So we went over there, and I got on my knees and said, "Will you marry me? I want you as my wife for the rest of my life."

All of a sudden she said, "Yes."

Right then a conference was breaking up, and they were seeing me kneeling down on my leg. Everyone started clapping and cheering, and everyone was whistling and celebrating with us.

We just turned beet red! So it was quite a incredible evening.

Hallie, she has epilepsy. When she was about a year and a half old, she had a blood clot that caused her epilepsy to explode. Her first grand mal seizure was at a year and a half, and it lasted for two hours. From then on, she had seizures.

There was a period when the family thought that she might be autistic, because what she end up doing is always banging her head up against the wall trying to hurt herself all the time. That didn't help the seizure-thing situation.

Her mother really trained her — holding her down and saying, "Look at me: You're not going to bang your head on the wall."

Hallie's mother did that for a long time. Then all of a sudden, Hallie quit doing it. It was because of the training when her mother would look in her eyes, hold her, and say, "You are not going to bang your head on the wall." And she snapped out of it.

Hallie had a very hard time being able to be touched; she didn't like to be touched at all.

Now you can't get her off of anybody; she touches all the time. It's just incredible. She gives hugs and everything else. It's just the opposite of what she was when she was growing up. She's a person with a lot of love.

She doesn't have the real high school diploma; she has the certificate saying she completed the hours of high school. She had a lot of tears about that, a lot of feelings about that. She was put into junior high, into a mainstream situation of general education, and she didn't last in it. There for a while, she was seizure-free. Then one day she got in an argument with the teacher, and she had another big seizure. It was seizures since then. She had medication that helped to control the seizures, and that did wonders.

After I asked her, I told her, "Lookit. You got to be able to move down to Sacramento; I'm tired of driving the mountain roads."

She called a 'partment complex, found out how much rent was, and she moved. Then after the move, we got into planning the wedding. Hallie's epilepsy just skyrocketed; it was just too much for her. We decided not to have all the bridesmaids and the best man and ushers. We were going to have it, but then it got just too much. Hallie was going crazy with her epilepsy, so we just had her sister stand up for the bridesmaid and my brother as the best man. It was a lot of work, and we were overwhelmed by the work.

There was one big issue: Her grandmom wanted to be able to have the wedding in her senior complex — a retirement home that she was living in. It was in Laguna Hills, and it was a really fancy clubhouse with a really fancy lawn. They thought that we could have it outdoors; but we didn't like it, because there was a flagpole in the middle of the yard, and the sun was in your eyes and it would be just too hot. So we decided to have it inside of the clubhouse.

It was just incredible — just one of the most beautiful weddings I ever seen in my life. The flowers were incredible; the food was awesome; the people were overwhelmed by their experience of being there.

It was really interesting. The night of the wedding rehearsal, a bunch of stuff got ripped off in Hallie's mother's car. It was candy and crayons and coloring books for all the children who couldn't sit through a wedding, and our cake knives got taken. So we had to have other cake knives to cut the cake. I didn't find that out until the cake was cut. They kept it pretty secretly. Thank goodness they did, because I probably would have hit the roof.

Hallie was Jewish, and her rabbi had a hard time to be able to have a Protestant minister do my part of the vows. So we had to go out and get a judge to make both sides happy. One of the interesting things that I found out later was the judge was a Jewish judge. It didn't particularly hurt me at all, because he was an incredible guy. I mean, I wouldn't want anybody else. If we had to have a judge, I wouldn't want any other judge to marry me, because he was a great guy.

One of the things that happened, though, was he forgot to send the marriage license back to Sacramento County. He thought that we were going to do that. We almost had to go down to get remarried at the county office, because everything was done wrong. We got a special waiver through the judge, saying that it was his mistake, and they did get married on this day and so on.

One thing I liked about Hallie is that she was really flexible. I had to be careful, not taking advantage of that flexibility. She liked that the decisions be made on my side, and if I fail, it's my fault! She didn't want to take no accountability of making mistakes. So that's why we had to be careful. But I thought that one of these days Hallie's going to get enough pride to be able to be assertive and say, "Lookit. It's going to happen this way." And she did begin to come out and do that. And I was glad, you know. It was only right and it was only healthy.

Before I got married, from August of 1992 to July of 1993, I was working seventeen days out on the road out of the twenty-two working days in a month. It was a schedule like a governor or a president. After I got married in July of '93, it went down to eight to twelve days a month out on the road.

April of 1992 is when I got off of Social Security. I turned myself in to Social Security and told them that I got a new job, and I don't need Social Security, because I make too much. I got my job and a car in the same month. Hallie and I started talking about a house, and we really started looking seriously in October. It took six months; we finally closed it in March the fourth, 1995. What made a difference in my life was the responsibilities that I took on as a person with a developmental disability.

It was a really great situation. I was calming down and starting to smell the roses, instead of being gone all the time and being grumpy when I come home. I think we had a much more happier life for a while. But working at the Department I didn't know how to be able to separate work from home life. I became a workaholic and that created problems in our marriage, so we decided to be able to go our separate ways.

* * *

The point to close with is how life takes us down to a journey of making fun of people; then when they all grow up, they realize all the mistakes they made as children.

There are specifically five people. These people were in my elementary and junior high years. I grew up all the time with them in the situation of where they always picked on me and always gave me a bad time.

Allen was one of them. Allen really changed a lot in the freshman year — really trying to get to know me. Kindergarten through eighth grade, Allen picked on me. And then what happened is one day the bus driver said, "You gotta knock it off and get to know Michael." So he changed his attitude because of the bus driver. And throughout high school he was always there for me, being able to encourage me to do things a lot more. When I was sick in the hospital, Allen sent me a card, where he would have never done that in the elementary years. He changed in a lot of ways by just acknowledging that he was wrong all those years of giving me a bad time. Now Allen and I ... we are the best friends that you can ever believe. Unbelievable is the friendship that me and Allen have. He has sent me Christmas cards. When I was sick, he tried to make a special trip to see me. It didn't work out, but just trying to put the effort into being able to do that meant a lot to me.

In one of his Christmas letters, he was saying, "Mike, you have really blown off my socks; I never believed that you would achieve all the things that you have achieved. Here you are; you're ahead of my life: I don't have a house; you beat me to getting married. You just should be grateful and thankful for all the things that you have accomplished."

That's the totally opposite. That was not Allen when he was in kindergarten all the way up to seventh-eighth grade. I mean, it's amazing.

Sabrina was one of them also, one of the females — the eighth-grade story of beating me up. At the class reunion, she came up to me and gave me the biggest hug and the biggest kiss that I ever received — besides my wedding day. She just was changed in the situation of so encouraging and so down to earth.

She said, "What is going on with you? I hear you've been really successful." It was just a really incredible difference. I didn't go to high school with her, because she went to a private high school, Mercy High school, a Catholic high school that was in Red Bluff area. So I didn't really see her at all in high school. Between high school and the class reunion when I ran into her, she always came up and talked to me like at the grocery store or at a movie.

Then there was Karen. She was a person in my class in grade school. In the sixth grade, then worse in the seventh grade, she was a leader and made the group give me a hard time. Of course looks and everything mattered to her. During 1981 to 1984, there was a period there where I ran into her when I still was living at home.

She gave me hugs, and she sit down and asked, "What are you doing?" and "What's going on in your life? We gotta get together. Let's get together sometime and go out and have a cup of coffee."

So a whole totally different attitude, which really got me excited. In eighth grade, I did kind of have a crush on Karen because of the way she looked. She was very good-looking, so I put all of that other stuff aside and fantasized and whatever you do in eighth grade.

Then there was Ted, where the bus driver sat down and made a difference in his life. "Hey, just go up and talk to him; he's no different than you are," the bus driver said.

Ted's been all over. He graduated from UC Berkeley, and then he went back to U of Yale and got his art degree. Ted has included me in everything. He ran into to me during the period of 1981-84. Then from 1986-91 we run into each other all the time, and we went out and did things together. We even got closer at the time when my dad died in 1991; then his father passed away and we got reacquainted again — being able to go out and talk to each other and everything. So he was just an incredible turnaround.

All of us grew up during the years. We knew we needed to be able to start better friendships, and communication, and support each other, and be there for each other. How that came about was by being separated.

And it's different than the seventh and eighth grade for me and my foster sister, Barbara. Our relationship became dramatically incredible when we grew up. We went out to dinner and had each other over, and now we are so close to each other. How incredible ... the changes of all these five people.

* * *

How could we sum it up? I needed support to be able to get where I got. To be able to get all of these friendships back into adulthood. I needed support. The support was to encourage me that I am capable and willing to do things. To be able to achieve these things, to be able to have a life like anybody else — like a non-disabled person — to have that American dream, to have the house, to be able to get married and to be able to accept myself ... who I am. All this came from the self-improvement course I took.

To be able to achieve the American dream it's a three-step process. That process is to be able to forgive those people who have done a lot of damage in your life, as when you were growing up in the elementary and high school years. That's the first step.

The second step is to be able to forgive yourself. You don't have any control; you don't have any control at all being disabled. You did not choose to be able to come into this world being disabled. You gotta be able to accept yourself as who you are and be able to acknowledge that and be able to forgive yourself of all of the things that you think — all of the negative things that you thought about yourself.

The third step is being able to overcome all of those things and to get a wish list of American dreams that you want to be able to have; and then build your domain of support of people who believe in you, and being able to believe that you have a chance to be able to achieve anything that you want to achieve in your life.

ABOUT THE AUTHORS

Michael S. Long attended California public schools before the Right to Education Act. He was the first person with an intellectual disability to be hired by a state government, when California Governor Pete Wilson appointed him as the Consumer Coordinator at the Department of Developmental Services in 1992.

Karl Williams has published two books with leaders in the self-advocacy movement, the civil rights work of people with intellectual disabilities. His play, based on one of these, *Lost in a Desert World: The Autobiography of Roland Johnson*, premiered in San Diego. Williams' third book, *Hello, Stranger* by Barbara Moran (as told to Williams), was published by KiCam Projects in 2019.

www.ingramcontent.com/pod-product-compliance
Lightning Source LLC
Chambersburg PA
CBHW070428010526
44118CB00014B/1955